Katherine Thompson has done the church and the [ ] *writing this book. Mindfulness is everywhere – scl* [ ] *book, the strengths and weaknesses of mindfulne:* [ ] *looked at respectfully and honestly. A very balanced, yet creative* [ ] *is outlined that builds on the best of mindfulness. A must read for those committed to Christian meditation and taking our faith into the marketplace where such spiritual disciplines abound.*

— Ross Clifford
Principal, Morling College

Katherine Thompson's call for Christ-centred mindfulness leads us to the place of contemplation where we can find ourselves and God. Quiet and meditative hearts seem rare these days. Our age is geared to speed and sound, but God cannot be easily seen or heard amid the noise and restlessness. The quest for inner peace seems both critical and difficult, and we need mindful silence to touch our souls. Quiet wisdom is what humanity desperately needs.

— Tim Costello
Chief Advocate, World Vision Australia

A timely and brilliantly practical book, Thompson brings her skills as a counsellor and her experience in analysing culture to the topic to help people ask the right questions to decide whether Christian mindfulness is the right thing for them and if so, how to take it up it in a Christ-centred way. She has written a guide that will be helpful for Christians in everyday life, for reinvigorating spiritual practices and for addressing those times of stress and pain in our lives.

— Tracy Lauersen
Senior Associate Vicar, St Hilary's Anglican Church, Kew, Melbourne

In Christ-Centred Mindfulness, *Dr Katherine Thompson demonstrates abiding faith and psychological rigour as she evaluates the historical and religious origins of mindfulness, and the complexities of employing mindfulness practices for believers today.*

Through biblically guided meditations and plenty of practical examples, Thompson capably illustrates how Christ-centred mindfulness can be employed as a psychologically informed practice of faith, not just acceptable to the Christian faith, but valuable and harmonious.

— Kylie Maddox Pidgeon
Registered Psychologist

For many of us, the world is full of spiritual complexity and ambiguity intersecting with our everyday. Spiritually loaded practices of positive psychology, meditation and yoga impact on our workplaces and our exercise choices. Mindfulness is increasingly being offered as a therapeutic solution to ailments, and to increase our enjoyment of life. In Christ-Centred Mindfulness *Katherine Thompson skilfully explains where mindfulness originated, how it is being used therapeutically, and where it fits in a biblical framework and in the Christian tradition. In doing this, she provides a wonderful model of engaging biblically and critically with our world. The Christian mindfulness exercises in Part III provide a useful alternative to any practices we might feel focus on self rather than on Jesus. This is an intelligent, well-researched and wise book.*

— Kara Martin
Author, Project Leader with Seed
and Lecturer at Mary Andrews College

This book provides a fantastic overview of the religious influences behind the current mindfulness craze. This kind of work is utterly missiological – providing an honest appraisal of the merits (and also the drawbacks) of a contemporary issue in order to allow Christians to form responses, sort through ideas, and engage the world around them. The beauty of this book is its willingness to adapt in order to promote psychologically sound principles, even while refusing the temptation to appropriate another's culture for one's own profit. The author undertakes the difficult task of returning back to the ancient Christian ways in order to promote wellbeing and good mental health amongst contemporary Christians. This kind of reflexive, resourceful and self-aware Christian is exactly what the world needs right now.

— Tanya Riches
Worship Leader, Theology Lecturer and Researcher

Christ Centred Mindfulness

CONNECTING TO SELF AND GOD

Katherine Thompson

ACORN PRESS

Published by Acorn Press

An imprint of Bible Society Australia ACN 148 058 306

GPO Box 9874

Sydney NSW 2001

Australia

www.acornpress.net.au | www.biblesociety.org.au

© 2018 Katherine Thompson

ISBN: 978-0-9946166-7-8 (paperback)

      978-0-9946166-8-5 (ebook)

A catalogue record for this
book is available from the
NATIONAL LIBRARY OF AUSTRALIA
National Library of Australia

Unless otherwise indicated, Scripture quotations are from the New Revised Standard Version Bible, copyright © 1989 the Division of Christian Education of the National Council of the Churches of Christ in the United States of America. Used by permission. Scripture quotations marked 'NIV' are taken from The Holy Bible, New International Version®, NIV® Copyright © 1973, 1978, 1984, 2011 by Biblica, Inc.™ Used by permission. All rights reserved worldwide.

Editor: Gina Denholm.

Cover design: Patrick Knowles.

Design and text layout: Shiloh Longbottom.

Contents

List of Abbreviations

ACT   acceptance and commitment therapy

CBT   cognitive behavioural therapy

DBT   dialectical behaviour therapy

MBCT mindfulness-based cognitive therapy

MBSR mindfulness-based stress reduction

Introduction
The Mindfulness Maze

In recent years, interest in the idea and practice of mindfulness has exploded. Mindfulness is about living in the now. In the area of counselling and mental health, it has been widely adopted as part of therapeutic treatment. This has trickled down into popular psychology and everyday health advice. A search for mindfulness titles on Amazon turns up hundreds of pages of books, DVDs and course materials, all promising to reveal the 'five core skills' or 'twenty top benefits' of mindfulness practice. And it's now the norm to find a mindfulness course at your local community centre.

Mindfulness has wide appeal. In popular culture, it is marketed as a way to achieve psychological wellbeing by making us feel better. A practice that takes a few minutes per day seems like an easy and promising fix to life's problems, especially if it makes us feel great in the process. It seems like the perfect antidote to the frantic pace of our society, which constantly bombards us with excesses of information and demand.

Mindfulness practice has become a self-administered form of therapy, easily accessible by anyone, anywhere. On my smartphone, I can now choose from numerous different mindfulness and meditation apps. The most popular app in Australia is *Smiling Mind*, developed by a not-for-profit organisation of the same name. *Smiling Mind* has a vision to make mindfulness meditation part of the Australian school curriculum by 2020, with the ultimate aim to make mindfulness meditation accessible everywhere, including the workplace.[1]

But where has mindfulness come from, and what is its core message? Much of the mindfulness taught in our society is a form of meditation that has come from Buddhist religious practice. These Buddhist roots are not always evident because the practice has been repackaged and mixed with popular psychology to give it credibility. It is thus defined in a number of ways. According to John Kabat-Zinn, mindfulness advocate and developer of mindfulness-based stress reduction, 'mindfulness means paying attention in a particular way: on purpose, in the present moment, and non-judgmentally.'[2]

This definition only really scratches the surface. Other questions need to be asked. Where did the concept of mindfulness arise? Does it work, and if so, how? Is it backed by evidence? For Christians, the questions go a little further. We've heard that mindfulness practices come from Buddhist roots, and we have been given conflicting opinions about how to engage with it. Should we take up mindfulness meditation when our doctor recommends it to reduce stress? Should we do that mindfulness course at work – the one the boss is recommending to increase productivity? Should we download that meditation app that promises to help us sleep better? What do we do when our kids come home from school and say they were taught mindfulness without our consent?

And if we do engage with mindfulness practices, are there ways to do this consistently with our Christian worldview? What about our own

---

1 *Smiling Mind*, 'Who We Are'.
2 Kabat-Zinn, *Wherever You Go*, p. 4.

faith heritage – does it have anything to offer us that could enrich our prayer lives, help us to draw near to God and grow in Christlikeness?

As someone who has worked in the area of mental health for nearly twenty years, as both a mental health researcher and counsellor, I've become increasing unsettled about the wide and indiscriminate adoption of mindfulness practice. Very few people are asking the right questions; even counsellors rarely stop to think about how mindfulness became so popular and why it is suddenly an accepted part of treatment.

For the past couple of years, therefore, I've been winding my way through the mindfulness maze. These are some of the questions that have surfaced:

- Where is the evidence for whether mindfulness works?
- What does it do to our brain?
- What kind of change are we encouraging in people?
- How does this change impact people spiritually?
- Can deep emotional problems be solved by short daily meditation?
- If the most common forms of mindfulness are actually Buddhist meditation, should they be taught to those who have a different faith or set of beliefs? Is that respectful of their culture and faith?

While asking these questions, my aim has not been merely to critique the potential pitfalls of mindfulness-based techniques, but also to examine healthy ways that Christians can engage with similar styles of practice. I have seen that there is clearly a benefit to practices that help us connect with the present moment and become fully engaged in life.

I have come to understand mindfulness as a way of using all our senses, and the quiet part of our mind, to connect well to both our internal and external world. Such mindfulness does not need to be rooted in Buddhist meditation, but can be based in Christian practices such as silence, rest and prayer. These things help us slow down, connect to what is happening inside ourselves and make space to listen for God's guiding in everyday life. This can produce a practice that is deeply embedded in faith values, bringing greater transformation, Christlikeness and a sense of fulfilment. We can become less stressed and anxious, and more able to respond to what is happening 'now' in a healthier way. Such spiritual growth cannot be achieved in five superficial minutes per day, but through disciplined habits that need to be tended to and integrated into life to create healthy change.

It is surprising that the church and Christian therapists have been slow to respond to the growing secular interest in mindfulness meditation. Even though there has been some rediscovery of Christian meditation and contemplative prayer practice, this knowledge is only held and practised by a relatively small number of people. It is not practised in the mainstream church, Catholic or Protestant.

A measured dialogue and response is needed, because there is much that could to be said in this space. A number of Christian books have recently been published in this area, but they either provide practical exercises, explaining what the present moment is and how it relates to faith, or apply mindfulness techniques to prayer.[3] None of these books take a deep look at the Buddhist roots of mindfulness-based practice, how it became part of mental health treatment, whether it works and how it may or may not fit with Christian faith.

---

3 Rohr, *The Naked Now*; Stead, *Mindfulness and Christian Spirituality*; Welch, *How To Be a Mindful Christian*.

I've therefore written this book to provide a carefully considered Christian response to the use of popular mindfulness. My purpose is to:

- explore where mindfulness comes from
- evaluate whether it assists with improving mental health
- critique its place in therapy and counselling
- offer practical exercises to encourage mindful connection to self and God that are compatible with a Christian perspective.

If you're a Christian who, like me, is curious about mindfulness practice but wants to think it through carefully, this book is for you. Or perhaps you work as a psychologist, counsellor or social worker and are trying to sort through your own approach to mindfulness-based therapies; while this book is written for a general audience, you may find it helpful for you or your clients. My hope is that this book will become a resource and encouragement for everyday people who want to increase their psychological flexibility and wellbeing by integrating mindful living into their daily life as part of their Christian spirituality.

Part I, 'Navigating Popular Mindfulness', aims to provide a well-considered Christian response to mindfulness. It examines how mindfulness-based interventions drawn from Buddhism can be measured against a Christian worldview and compares one particular therapy, acceptance and commitment therapy (ACT), with components of Christian contemplative spirituality in order to define what Christ-centred mindfulness could look like.

Part II, 'Exploring Christian Roots', goes deeper into the idea of Christ-centred mindfulness by looking at contemplative strands in the Bible. It then engages with our rich history of contemplative practice from the Christian mystic tradition (both ancient and modern) and explores the similarities these share with ACT.

The greater purpose of this book is to move beyond discussion and theory and into practice. Part III, 'Practising Christ-Centred Mindfulness', provides practical mindfulness exercises that are rooted in Scripture, the Christian mystic tradition and ACT.

I encourage you to read sections of this book as they are relevant to you. If you want to, it is possible to skip the theory and go straight to practising the exercises provided in the last part of the book.

My greatest hope is that, in reading this book, you will be able to navigate the mindfulness maze with confidence and learn how to connect with God and with yourself – through *Christ-centred* mindfulness.

PART I

Navigating Popular Mindfulness

1

Critically Contextualising Mindfulness

The dialogue between faith and daily living is complex. Christians take different approaches to the task of evaluating cultural practices and their compatibility with faith. Some of us prefer to rely solely on what is written in Scripture as a measure of what God says and ignore Christian tradition, personal experience of God or things of cultural importance. This can sometimes result in unthinking rejection of cultural practices. This is a missed opportunity, because it can isolate us from what is happening around us and make our beliefs and message seem literal, inflexible, alien and irrelevant to other people.

The opposite can also be true. We can uncritically live within the values of our own culture or inadvertently absorb secular and other religious thinking without considering whether these ideas are consistent with our faith. In so doing, we risk being indiscriminate by assimilating with those values and worldviews. For many Christians in the West, this is perhaps a bigger concern than outright rejection.

Because the Christian faith is governed by broad principles and not vast sets of laws, there is a great deal of freedom for believers in how we interact with our culture. But as Paul reminds the Corinthian Christians, who so loved to abuse their freedoms, "'All things are lawful", but not all things are beneficial. "All things are lawful", but not all things build up' (1 Cor 10:23). Paul also speaks to the Christians in Rome, who were arguing over cultural practices of which foods they could eat and which days were sacred, reminding them that they need to accept the one whose faith is weak without quarrelling over disputable matters (Rom 14:1). He goes on to say that whatever we decide is between each person and God, and we will be judged for that decision. At the same time, we are warned not to do anything that causes another person to doubt or question their own faith practice.

As Christians, we therefore need to be discerning about how we engage with the culture around us. Absorbing ideas and practices into our lives that are inconsistent with the teachings of Christ risks watering down our faith. Jesus wants us to be the 'salt of the earth' and warns us not to lose our saltiness in the world (Lk 14:34). The challenge is to work out how our faith in God informs our worldview and values and determines what sort of people we need to be and how we are going to live our lives.

Within our own culture of origin, we can find it hard to think critically about cultural beliefs and practices because we have become dulled to them. The need to be thoughtful about the relationship between faith and culture is more obvious when we're in a cross-cultural situation. I found this when I went as part of a team to live in Kazakhstan for 18 months. During this time, my fellow team members and I had to grapple with how much the Kazakh identity was shaped by Islamic faith, and how much by culture. For those who do not know much about this former Soviet country, faith and identity are a messy integration of ancient animistic practices, shamanism, Islam and Soviet communism. As Islam did not really take hold among these traditionally nomadic people until more recently, most Kazakhs are only nominally Muslim and do not attend the mosque regularly or pray five times per day.[1] Women do not have any particular dress requirement and are often more liberal in their fashion than we would be in Australia. Day to day, people are more concerned about the evil eye and needing protection from evil spirits. It is normal to pray a blessing on another person, hands open, in a public area.

The last thing we wanted to do was impose our Western ideas of faith on these people. We needed to consider what it might mean for people in this context to be a follower of Christ. Christine Mallouhi writes that it is possible to be both a follower of Christ and retain Islamic culture.[2] The point of difference is that each part of that culture needs to be measured against Christ's teaching. Anything that is not contradictory can be kept. The thinking is that it is better to be a follower of Christ in this context by retaining some cultural practices than by unthinkingly abandoning them and becoming completely separated from family, community and identity as a result.

The need to contextualise our faith is not merely a modern issue. The early church faced frequent challenges of how to integrate faith and culture. For example, they grappled with tensions between Jewish and gentile believers and had to decide whether gentile followers of Christ needed to be circumcised (Acts 15; Galatians). The Apostle Paul worked to help the Corinthian Christians think through how to relate to its cultural context – for example, whether to participate in eating food sacrificed to idols (1 Corinthians). Other fledgling

---

1 Lewis, *After Atheism*.
2 Mallouhi, *Miniskirts, Mothers and Muslims*.

churches needed help to figure out how to articulate and live out their faith in the face of the growing influence of Gnosticism, which had a dualistic view of the world (see 1 John). In all of these cases, the early church had to consider the cultural ideas and practices around them through the lens of the Christian faith.

In the same way, contemporary Christians need to learn how to critically evaluate ideas that come from our own societies and cultures. (In this book, I am writing to Christians in Western, industrialised societies and cultures, although the concept is equally applicable to other cultures.)

This is vital for Christians who are seeking counselling, therapy or treatment and trying to discern if practices such as mindfulness meditation will be helpful or harmful to their faith.

The purpose of this chapter is to help us to 'contextualise' mindfulness – that is, to understand what it means within our cultural context and to see how this relates to our faith. First, we'll take a deeper look at the ideas of worldview and contextualisation. Next, we will look specifically at the Buddhist concept of mindfulness and think about how it does, and doesn't, fit with a Christian worldview.

WORLDVIEW AND CONTEXTUALISATION

Worldview is a term used by anthropologists to describe how we understand and see the world. It is the lens through which we view everything in our experience: the way we interact with and interpret our environment, how we feel about it and the thoughts we have about it. It is not necessary to have a religious belief to have a worldview, but for many people faith is one aspect that informs the way they see the world.

Our worldview shapes the way we categorise our experiences and the assumptions we make about them. It determines whom we trust

Figure 1.1. Worldview (adapted from Hiebert).[3] Our worldview is based on our individual inner thoughts, feelings and evaluations, and these determine our explicit beliefs and values. As a collective group of people we can view the world in a similar way, and share some of the same beliefs and values, and this shapes the outward working of our social institutions.

and how we think about things (see Figure 1.1). On an affective level, it influences what music we like, how we dress, the kind of buildings we live in and use, and how we feel towards other people and life in general. We evaluate our world so that we have a standard of comparison, which helps us determine what is truth, what we like and what we see as right. These evaluations help us prioritise what is important in our culture.

When we move from the individual to the community, the worldview of the majority determines how families and groups interact as well as their laws and government. It determines artistic expression, the way money is used and how technology is used to advance society. These collective aspects of worldview make up what we refer to as our culture.

When we apply this understanding of worldview to Western culture, we can see the various influences that have shaped our social institutions and the way our society functions. In Australia, for example, Judeo-Christian religion has influenced the ethics of our legal and justice systems. Economic rationalism and capitalism influence the functioning of our economy. Democracy is the dominant value in our structure and style of government. Where once our collective religion and faith primarily aligned with the Christian church, now

---

3 Hiebert, *Anthropological Insights for Missionaries*, p. 46.

our culture is increasingly secular in nature. Religion has become individualistic and multicultural and exerts less influence on society.

These values and ways we have organised our culture stem from changes that occurred during the Enlightenment, and they have dominated much of Western thought since the eighteenth century. Values we have unknowingly adopted from this period form the basis of modern thinking (Figure 1.2). These include the rise of science as truth and the understanding of religion as private, individualised faith. Another important modern idea is the belief in human progress, which underpins our thinking that we need to continue to improve and develop things.

In contrast, postmodernism is a reaction against the influence of modernity in Western society (Figure 1.3). It has tried to challenge the basis of some of the assumptions we hold. It places greater importance on personal values over scientific rationalism, and it has prompted a renewed interest in forms of spirituality that are not grounded in mainstream institutionalised religion. This has helped our society see that science and history are influenced by issues of power and motivation and need to be challenged rather than taken as fact. It has made us take stock of the connection between our lifestyle and our physical and mental wellbeing.

The downside to postmodern thinking is that values and beliefs have become more relativistic and individualistic and are no longer challenged. There is no longer any standard or accepted way to measure right and wrong. Spirituality is valued but not defined, and religion is rejected.

As followers of Christ, we live between two worldviews. The first worldview is our lived experience, seen through the eyes of our faith. The second worldview is the one we have grown up in and live in.

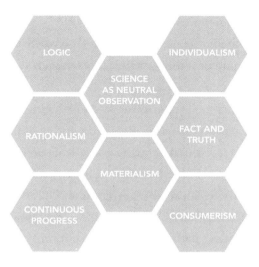

Figure 1.2. The values that form the foundation of a modern worldview

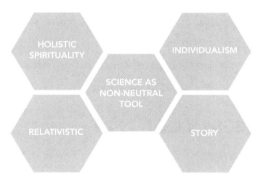

Figure 1.3. The values that form the foundation of a postmodern worldview

We become people of the middle ground – keeping everything that is consistent with our faith and rejecting the cultural values that are not in line with it. Doing this is anything but simple; the process challenges our beliefs to their core and asks us to determine what is both essential to and helpful for our faith.

For many of us today, worldview has developed even further complexity due to globalisation and migration between countries. For some of us, there may be a third or fourth worldview in play, shaping our personal perspective.

Given this complexity, it is tempting to adopt a kind of cultural relativism, where all worldviews and the values and belief systems they are built upon are judged to be equally good. But such a stance is not meaningful; it stops dialogue between cultures and, in its extreme form, leads to a disbelief in science, religion and all forms of knowledge.[4] It is nihilistic and makes life meaningless. As followers of Christ, we need to take another path and weigh up different cultures, beliefs and values according to Scripture and objective reality.[5] This reality extends to our own personal faith experience and the inherited traditions and practices of the church. In evaluating our faith against the practices of other people and cultures, a response is required. New knowledge is evaluated and either integrated in some way into our faith, or it is rejected as being inconsistent with it. This evaluation process is called critical contextualisation, and it produces transformation.

MINDFULNESS IN CONTEXT

Buddhist origins

The term 'mindfulness' has long been associated with Buddhism, and most people assume the term actually arose from Buddhism. Few people realise that in the West, the word 'mindfulness' was first used in 1530 in the context of Christian faith.[6] This is something we will delve into in later chapters. However, much of the interest in

---

4 Hiebert et al., *Understanding Folk Religion*, p. 21.

5 Ibid., p. 21.

6 Sun, 'Mindfulness in context', p. 395.

mindfulness in contemporary Western society is connected to Buddhist ideas, and so we must begin our contextualisation with understanding its Buddhist form.

In Buddhism, the English term, 'mindfulness', is drawn from the word *sati*, which is found in the Buddhist Scriptures.[7] It can be described as a 'presence of mind'. This word is closely related to the word *sarati*, which means 'to remember'.[8] These were traditionally translated in the West as 'conscience' and 'meditation'.[9] Together these terms refer to having a bare awareness of your inner and outer world in the present moment. It was not until around 1881 that the word mindfulness was first used as the English translation of the Buddhist concept of *sati*.[10]

Buddhism aims towards the elimination of suffering. It is based on the Four Noble Truths:

1. All life is suffering and pain.
2. Suffering is caused by selfish desire.
3. This selfishness can be overcome.
4. The way to do this is through the Eightfold Noble Path.

The Eightfold Noble Path is comprised of wisdom, ethics and meditation.[11] In its purest form, it uses radical inquiry to understand how things really are. It teaches that humans do not possess an eternal soul or self; rather, they are 'no-self'. Buddhism understands that everything in the world is interconnected. It values compassion, and aims towards the elimination of suffering, with the ultimate goal being liberation from the cycle of reincarnation.[12]

---

7 Chiesa & Malinowski, 'Mindfulness-based approaches', p. 405.
8 Ibid., p. 406.
9 Sun, 'Mindfulness in context', p. 396.
10 Ibid.
11 Dawson & Turnbull, 'Is mindfulness the new opiate for the masses?'.
12 Sun, 'Mindfulness in context', p. 396.

In Buddhism, the aim of mindfulness meditation is to achieve insight into and freedom from suffering. It seeks to balance the mind and emotions to produce a state of serenity and peacefulness. In its purer form, different stages of meditation and mindfulness are practised, like focusing attention on an object, observing thoughts and feelings, serving others, guarding others through your own patience and loving-kindness, eradicating bad habits, and attaining happiness or enlightenment.[13]

Western adaptation

In recent decades, mindfulness has made its way into our modern Western culture. This began in the realm of psychology, where mindfulness meditation practices have been separated from Buddhism and adapted for use in therapy, using language that is more accessible to the everyday person. Indeed, the mindfulness exercises contained in three of the four mindfulness-based psychological interventions are grounded in these Buddhist meditative practices, and we'll take a closer look at these in the next chapter. This focus on mindfulness, rather than Buddhist meditation, is also reflected in an exponential increase of academic mindfulness-based publications: these numbered less than 76 before 1990, compared to over 2705 between 2010 and 2014.[14] This rapid increase bears no relation to the number of Buddhist publications in the same period, which has remained relatively consistent. [15]

The question is whether this simplified form of mindfulness is a skilful *re*contextualisation of Buddhist teachings by religious proponents, or whether it is a secular *de*contextualisation that has divorced the prac-

---

13 Chiesa & Malinowski, 'Mindfulness-based approaches'.
14 Sun, 'Mindfulness in context', p. 402.
15 Ibid.

tice from its ethical and religious roots, separating it from the wisdom and ethics of the Eightfold Noble Path.

An element of recontextualisation is likely. Buddhism tends to be syncretistic when it spreads to other cultures, building on elements of indigenous beliefs that were already present so that it is more appealing to people of other faiths.[16] Some Zen masters believe that a health-related motivation to engage in mindfulness does not necessarily pose a problem, because they hope that, over time, people who practise these techniques will have less attachment to this initial motivation and move towards the deeper Buddhist teaching that undergirds mindfulness.[17]

On the whole, however, the adaptation of mindfulness to the Western context appears to be more likely a product of decontextualisation, where Western practitioners have separated mindfulness techniques from their Buddhist framework in order to use these methods to improve health and wellbeing. This has been the overt intention of practitioners such as Kabat-Zinn, the founder of MBSD.[18] It could be argued, therefore, that psychological theories that use mindfulness have not invented a new therapy tool so much as repackaged Buddhist mindfulness meditation without its former religious strings attached. The end result is a secular, humanistic distortion of the original concept, devoid of the depth of meaning and significance that it originally had. Some have called this 'McMindfulness'.[19]

This recent secular distortion has not gone entirely unnoticed, although the voices of dissent remain surprisingly few. Some Buddhist psychotherapists have called into question the way that mod-

16 Ibid, p. 404..
17 Chiesa & Malinowski, 'Mindfulness-based approaches'.
18 Kabat-Zinn, 'Mindfulness-based interventions in context'.
19 Sun, 'Mindfulness in context', p. 406.

ern psychology has extracted mindfulness practice from Eastern religion and separated it from the deeper values of Buddhist ethics.[20] They comment that the benefits of mindfulness to psychological health are not in dispute; rather, the ideas that underpin Buddhist mindfulness are missing. Their main concern is that mindfulness will become just another psychological technique used to reduce distress without addressing the deep cause of this suffering. It potentially leads to only superficial calmness, and it might have the function of being an opiate for Western society.[21] It will not necessarily lead to personal change.

What has happened in practice is the mindfulness found in Buddhism has been adapted to fit the Western modern worldview. As we discovered earlier, Buddhism's aim is to eliminate suffering, with the ultimate goal being liberation from the cycle of reincarnation. In contrast, Western modernity is rationally orientated towards productivity, profit and efficiency.[22] It values facts and objective truth. An object is assigned worth according to its cost effectiveness. This value functions alongside neo-liberalism, consumerism and individualism. These values have produced distortions in our society – we have now become more narcissistic, so that we see the value of everything in terms of how it can meet our own self-need.[23] Divorcing mindfulness from its Buddhist roots and merging it with psychology is an example of just this type of narcissistic distortion.

It is apparent that mindfulness meditation has become another commodity that our Western culture uses to improve itself to get ahead. It has become self-centred, a personal possession that can be

20 Dawson & Turnbull, 'Is mindfulness the new opiate for the masses?'
21 Ibid.
22 Ibid.
23 Twenge, *The Narcissism Epidemic.*

used for our own end to get relief from physical and psychological symptoms. Divorced from its true context, it is devoid of any significant meaning.

A problematic divorce

With the rise of postmodern thought, Western contemporary society is becoming more syncretistic. While modernism has contributed to the way that the West has turned mindfulness into a commodity, in many ways the current resurgence of mindfulness in our society is a postmodern Western response to that same rational thought. In postmodernism, there is a tendency to incorporate ideas from different sources without critique and reflection. Cherrypicking from the Buddhist faith makes sense within a postmodern perspective, where values and beliefs are considered relative. In this context, it is not surprising that mindfulness-based psychological interventions have become popular.

A non-critical response, however, is not adequate in the context of faith. As Christians who want to carefully consider cultural practices in light of our faith, we need to critique the way that Western culture has unthinkingly adapted Buddhist meditation practices for therapeutic use.

First, there is the issue of disrespecting or misrepresenting the Buddhist framework from which mindfulness practices have been extracted. While this may not seem like a large consideration for those of us who do not hold to a Buddhist worldview, consider how you would react if psychologists started adapting the Christian sacramental rites of Baptism or the Lord's Supper for therapeutic use but emptied them of their original meaning.

Second, we need to ask ourselves whether such practices are as benign as they appear. History provides some warning about how adapting mindfulness practices can result in destructive distortion. In World War II, for example, the Japanese merged nationalism with mindfulness, employing mindfulness techniques in what they called a 'Holy War'. The military received Zen training in mindfulness, or 'zazen', so that it became combat zazen. This harmful adaptation of mindfulness practice was aimed at enhancing the capacity of soldiers to concentrate in order to kill, and to do this serenely and unquestioningly.[24]

While we might not consider that this distortion could occur in our own society, to some extent it already has. Organisations use mindfulness to reduce stress and boost the productivity of their workers. Here in Australia, secondary school students are encouraged to learn mindfulness so that they optimise their exam performance. And, perhaps more disturbingly, the US military have adopted mindfulness practice into their training so they can optimise combat performance.[25] When mindfulness becomes a mere tool, unbound from any ethical injunctions or a wider moral framework, it has potential to be dangerous.

Finally, Christians need to be wary of adopting the practices of other religions that can open the door to harmful spiritual influence. Both prayer and mindfulness use the quiet part of our mind. If prayer opens us up to hearing God's Spirit, it therefore follows that mindfulness potentially opens us up to other spiritual influences. Even though this seems benign, it could prove to be harmful. This is one of the main concerns I have for people who unknowingly en-

---

24 Dawson & Turnbull, 'Is mindfulness the new opiate for the masses?', p.61.
25 Sun, 'Mindfulness in context', p. 406.

gage in popular mindfulness. Are they opening their mind to spirits they don't understand?

The influence of other religions can gradually lead us down the path of idolatry. We can see this tension and struggle between faith and culture in the Old Testament, in the example of Solomon. When he took over the throne from King David, he 'loved the LORD, walking in the statutes of his father David' (1 Kgs 3:3) and God blessed him with great wisdom and discernment (1 Kgs 3:8–9; 4:34). Over the span of his rule he built a great temple so that Judah and Israel could worship God. Their country experienced a time of peace and prosperity.

But as Solomon's forty-year reign continued, he adopted the cultural practice of intermarriage with foreign princesses – a practice common for kings in the ancient Near East, who used these marriages to strengthen political ties with surrounding nations. However, the Israelites had been warned against this practice because it could lead them into idolatry (1 Kgs 11:2). Gradually, this practice inclined Solomon's heart away from the God of Israel, and he followed the gods of his wives and stopped observing what the Lord had commanded (1 Kgs 11:1–11). So God tore his kingdom from him, and thereafter Judah and Israel were two separate kingdoms.

From then on, we see the history of Israel and Judah as fraught by a pattern of following God's ways, then drifting away to follow the gods of the nations around them, incurring God's wrath and repenting, and returning once again to worship their own God. The cycle continued, and it is an example to us of the importance of following God's ways and not totally assimilating with the beliefs of the people around us. Our God wants us to be fully devoted to him.

In the same way, it is wise for contemporary Christians to be cautious about wholeheartedly embracing mindfulness practices that stem from Buddhist roots. Paul says our bodies are the temple of the living God (2 Cor 6:14—7:1). We are to be separate from unbelievers and touch nothing that is unclean for both our body and spirit. We are to be holy and fear God. This means we will not engage in a practice that can open us up to spiritual harm or idolatry. We need to make wise choices. To uncritically assimilate Buddhist mindfulness practices into our daily lives can lead to syncretism, whereas a process of thoughtful evaluation can lead to healthy transformation.

To be people of the two worlds of faith and culture forces us to confront this issue and decide how we are going to respond. As in the example of Solomon, God wants us to follow his ways and not follow the teachings of other religions. Mindfulness meditation and inner transformation need to be based on Christian values so that we do not lose our saltiness but stand out as a light to the world.

2

Mindfulness, Psychology and Science

In the last chapter, we looked at the Buddhist origins of mindfulness teaching and concluded that Christians need to be prepared to engage critically with mindfulness therapies, questioning the worldview that mindfulness meditation arises from rather than unthinkingly accepting all elements of such a practice as beneficial. The reason for us to be cautious is that we want to avoid adopting syncretistic practices that conflict with our own worldview and can hinder our walk with God.

Given this, you might be wondering why I don't recommend walking away from all mindfulness practice together. Wouldn't it just be easier to avoid all mindfulness-based therapies? My answer is twofold.

First, we must address the misconception that mindfulness meditation is the sole possession of Buddhist practice. In fact, these practices exist in all of the main world religions – Buddhism, Hinduism, Judaism, Islam and Christianity. Such practices are usually found within the mystic traditions that inhabit each religion. In Christianity, these techniques have been used for hundreds of years and are enjoying a resurgence in recent times. We will explore this rich history in depth in Part II.

Second, we must acknowledge the mounting body of scientific evidence that mindfulness practice has proven benefits for mental health and human wellbeing. For example, people like myself who suffer severe chronic physical pain can broker a peace with their symptoms by living in a mindful way. Instead of expending energy on anxiously avoiding the pain, we can learn to be more accepting of it in order to maintain wellbeing. This can help us be less dependent on painkillers to obliterate our suffering. Mindful living that is guided by our values gives us the will and motivation to live a life that has meaning, every single day.

Like all other areas of scientific endeavour, we want to explore whether God can help us use such therapies for good and whether we can find a way to do so without compromising our core beliefs. And that's the purpose of this chapter. Here, we're going to take a look at the major mindfulness therapies currently in use and consider the scientific evidence for the benefits and effectiveness of mindfulness practice. This will help us think through which forms of mindfulness are most suited to Christian engagement.

MINDFULNESS IN PSYCHOLOGY: THE FOUR MAIN THERAPIES

Mindfulness has come to the forefront of mental health treatment and counselling with the emergence of a range of new therapies. Steven Hayes, one of the main proponents of ACT, has referred to these new therapies as third-generation approaches, extending behavioural therapy (first generation) and cognitive behavioural therapy (CBT; second generation).[1]

---

1 Hayes et al., 'Acceptance and commitment therapy', p. 2.

Behavioural therapy is based on the idea that our behaviour is acquired through conditioning and our interaction with the environment.

Cognitive behavioural therapy builds upon this first approach by arguing that our thoughts and behaviours contribute to the development of psychological disorders such as depression. If we change our maladaptive thinking, then this will change our behaviours and feelings. It is one of the most popular techniques used in counselling today.

The third-generation therapies include ACT, dialectical behaviour therapy (DBT), mindfulness-based cognitive therapy (MBCT) and MBSR. Hayes argues that these approaches are a third wave of cognitive therapy because they supersede behavioural therapy and CBT.[2] Not all professionals agree with his stance.[3] It is perhaps more correct to name them as postmodern extensions of CBT, with the exception of MBSR, which does not use any of the components of cognitive therapies as it is based solely on Buddhist meditation practices. The one thing all of these third-generation therapies have in common is that they include a component of connecting with the present moment, referred to as mindfulness or mindful connection to the present.

For the most part, again except for MBSR, mindfulness is used as only one aspect of these therapeutic models. Many of these therapies have been tested and found to show a range of benefits. They have been used in healthy people, those with chronic physical illness and people with a mental illness. The practice of mindfulness has been shown to have a measurable treatment effect that has been linked to changes in brain function.

---

2 Ibid.

3 Hoffman & Asmundson, 'Acceptance and mindfulness-based therapy', p. 12.

Mindfulness-based stress reduction

Mindfulness-based stress reduction was developed in the 1970s by Jon Kabat-Zinn at the University of Massachusetts Medical Centre. It is a treatment program that uses daily mindfulness meditation, where mindfulness is defined as 'the awareness that emerges through paying attention on purpose, in the present moment, and non-judgementally to the unfolding of experience moment by moment.'[4] It involves observing internal and external experience as it arises, and it can be practiced in any situation and during any activity.[5]

Mindfulness-based stress reduction is a structured therapy program delivered in a group setting. The program typically runs for a total of eight weeks. The group meets each week for between 1.5 and 2.5 hours, and for one whole day of silent retreat during week six. During the sessions, mindfulness meditation is taught and participants discuss their experience of it. Meditation exercises include mindful body scanning, sitting meditation, walking meditation and basic hatha yoga postures.[6] Participants are asked to practise these exercises daily for between 20 and 45 minutes, and to incorporate mindfulness into their daily activities.[7]

The original MBSR program was developed to assist people suffering from chronic pain and stress-related disorders. It has since been used to help people with a range of conditions including cancer, anxiety, psoriasis and eating disorders. Reviews of treatment studies have reported that MBSR can make chronic health condi-

---

4 Kabat-Zinn, 'Mindfulness-based interventions in context', p.145.
5 Merkes, 'Mindfulness-based stress reduction for people with chronic diseases'.
6 Sharma & Rush, 'Mindfulness-based stress reduction'.
7 Merkes, 'Mindfulness-based stress reduction for people with chronic diseases'.

tions easier to manage and cope with and improve general wellbeing and quality of life.[8] It improves mental health in healthy people and those with a mental illness,[9] as well as reducing the symptoms of anxiety and depression and associated distress.[10]

Mindfulness-based stress reduction is the therapy most closely linked to Buddhism.[11] It integrates Buddhist philosophy into its practice and is heavily influenced by Zen Buddhism. Sometimes during sessions, MBSR practitioners might read mindfulness scripts written by Buddhist authors. Even so, Kabat-Zinn, the founder of this therapeutic approach, states that people from other religions can still participate in these programs.[12] Mindfulness-based stress reduction is still marketed as a secular intervention even though it is overtly Buddhist in origin. It is the only psychological therapy that is mainly based on mindfulness practice alone.

Mindfulness-based cognitive therapy

Mindfulness-based cognitive therapy is often reviewed in conjunction with MBSR, as there are many similarities between these two approaches. For example, MBCT is also an eight-week, group-based program, which includes an all-day retreat and daily practice homework.[13] However, it differs from MBSR because it integrates elements of both CBT and Buddhist mindfulness meditation into treatment.[14]

---

8 Ibid.
9 Kloury et al., 'Mindfulness-based stress reduction for healthy individuals'.
10 Fjorback, 'Mindfulness-based stress reduction and mindfulness-based cognitive therapy'.
11 Chiesa & Malinowski, 'Mindfulness-based approaches'.
12 Ibid.
13 Van der Velden et al., 'A systematic review'.
14 Chiesa & Malinowski, 'Mindfulness-based approaches'.

First manualised in 2002,[15] it was developed to prevent relapse in people who had already experienced multiple episodes of depression.[16]

Reviews of this treatment have shown that mindfulness had a positive effect on treatment outcome because it was thought to reduce the amount of rumination and worry.[17] The risk of relapse of depression was also reduced.

The mindfulness component of this treatment, as with MBSR, is thought to work through increasing self-awareness, regulating attention and emotion, encouraging an accepting stance and facilitating cognitive change through decentring, which is a process of taking a step back from our thoughts and beliefs so that we don't have to believe all of them.[18]

Dialectical behaviour therapy

Marsha Linehan developed DBT for the treatment of borderline personality disorder in 1993.[19] This therapy is a form of cognitive behavioural treatment incorporating strategies that encourage acceptance and mindfulness. It is based on the biosocial theory of borderline personality disorder and openly affirms a dialectical worldview, which assumes that things are not black or white and aims to hold extremes in tension. The main influences of this approach are behavioural science, dialectical philosophy and Zen Buddhism.[20]

Dialectical behaviour therapy looks at the context of behaviour, together with the interrelatedness of individual behaviour. In this

---

15 Treatments are manualised in step-by-step format so that counsellors can use a guide to make sure they are keeping to the therapy and delivering it in a standard way.

16 Van der Velden et al., 'A systematic review'.

17 Ibid.

18 Gu et al., 'A systematic review and meta-analysis of meditation studies'.

19 Linehan, *Skills Training Manual*.

20 Chiesa & Malinowski, 'Mindfulness-based approaches'.

framework, people who are lacking essential life skills need to learn a whole set of skills simultaneously because one new skill is of limited utility on its own. Learning psychosocial skills is particularly challenging because a person's environment does not always support change. It can be useful to learn these skills, but a capacity to change other environmental influences is also needed. This therapy extends these concepts further by considering the concept of dialectics, where propositions have oppositions. People undertaking this treatment are discouraged from black-and-white thinking. Instead, they are encouraged to hold opposing thoughts in tension and work towards synthesis. The final aspect of dialectics assumes that change is an essential process and part of reality.[21]

This therapy has been manualised as a skills-based group program. It uses a wide range of cognitive and behavioural strategies for the treatment of borderline personality disorder. It emphasises four main areas:

- the acceptance and validation of behaviour in the moment
- the treatment of unhelpful behaviours arising from both clinician and patient that disrupt therapy progress
- the centrality of the therapeutic relationship in treatment
- the use of dialectical processes.

In this therapeutic approach, Linehan acknowledges that acceptance is necessary to create change and that this view of acceptance integrates Eastern spiritual practices into Western psychological treatment.[22] This skills-training program typically runs weekly, incorporating a homework feedback session and a skills-training session. The duration of therapy can be as long as one year. Topics covered include interper-

---

21 Linehan, *Skills Training Manual*.
22 Ibid.

sonal effectiveness, emotion regulation, distress tolerance and core mindfulness. This therapy is now accepted as an effective treatment for borderline personality disorder, and this approach has been used to treat a number of other forms of mental illness where emotional regulation is an issue.

Linehan states that the core mindfulness skills taught in DBT are 'psychological and behavioural versions of meditation practices from Eastern spiritual training.'[23] She draws most heavily upon the practice of Zen, but believes the skills are compatible with other forms of meditative practice.

In this DBT approach, three states of mind are recognised: reasonable mind, emotional mind and wise mind. Achieving wise mind is the goal of therapy, and it is the integration of both reasonable and emotional mind. Mindfulness skills taught in this approach are:

- observing events, emotions and behaviours
- describing events and personal responses in words
- the ability to enter completely into activities in the current moment.

In doing these things, it is important to maintain a non-judgemental stance, learn to focus the mind on what is happening in the current moment, and act in a way that is effective in the present.

Acceptance and commitment therapy

Acceptance and commitment therapy stems from CBT. It is based in functional contextualism, which considers that no thought, memory or feeling is a problem in and of itself, but rather depends on the context in which it occurs.[24] If we fuse with our thoughts (that

23 Ibid., p. 63.
24 Hayes et al., 'Acceptance and commitment therapy'.

is, absolutely believe them) and start to avoid thoughts, feelings and memories, this becomes toxic and distorts the way we live our life. In contrast, if we can defuse and accept the thoughts, feelings and memories (that is, let them be there and make space for them), then they have less power and influence over how we behave. This does not make them less painful, but they are no longer holding us back from living a life that we value.

The goal of functional contextualism is to predict and influence behaviour to help people to create full and meaningful lives and foster mindful living. Acceptance and commitment therapy teaches people to be more aware of their own behaviour and notice how it functions in the context of their life. It asks the question, does the behaviour improve your wellbeing and the quality of your life?

This philosophical standpoint is further expanded by relational frame theory.[25] This is a difficult concept, but it essentially means that human thinking is a learnt behaviour. The way we think about things is influenced by past experience and the context in which something occurred. For example, a teacher at school could tell you 'you are not good at mathematics.' If this had a huge impact on you at the time, you would be able to bring to mind what the classroom looked like, how you felt, what other people were saying and how they reacted around you. This one event is stored in your memory. It comes loaded with a complex mix of thoughts, feelings and sensory sensations. It can taunt you each time you have to work out a maths sum in everyday life. This layers your association with maths with a whole lot of other events and the associated memories of

---

25 Relational frame theory: 'The core of human language and cognition is the learned and contextually controlled ability to arbitrarily relate events mutually and in combination, and to change the functions of specific events based on their relations to others' (Hayes et al., 'Acceptance and commitment therapy', p. 5).

thoughts, feelings and sensations.

Our brain makes associations between such events, and this broadens our knowledge about ourselves. In our example, you could end up as an adult who totally believes that they cannot do maths. This will discourage you from taking up a profession that involves any number-related tasks; it could also sap your confidence for doing basic calculations in daily tasks such as budgeting and shopping. You might even avoid trying to do these tasks. Here we see that events are the ongoing actions of a person who is interacting both in and with a historical and situational context.[26]

To address relational frame theory, ACT seeks to increase psychological flexibility and help people respond in healthy ways to their thoughts and feelings so that their thoughts are not so unhelpfully deterministic. Instead, people are encouraged to see that actions and choices are based on their values, what kind of person they want to be and what is important to them.

This therapeutic approach builds on these assumptions using six core processes:

- using expansion to make room for unpleasant feelings
- defusing from difficult thoughts
- connecting to the present moment
- using the observing self as context for using mindfulness and metaphor
- clarifying core values
- taking committed action.

Mindful living in this context means connecting to the present moment, rather than reacting out of old thoughts and behaviours that take your mind away from living life in the now.

---

26 Hayes et al., 'Acceptance and commitment therapy'.

Acceptance and commitment therapy has been used for a number of different problems including depression, anxiety, post-traumatic stress disorder, stress and chronic pain. Reviews of treatment effectiveness report moderate effect sizes, which means there is evidence that this therapeutic approach works.[27] It has been shown to increase psychological flexibility and improve quality of life and outcomes for participants.[28]

Unlike the previous therapies discussed, proponents of ACT argue that the need for being focused in the present is based in the science and philosophy, or worldview, of functional contextualism and relational frame theory. Mindful connection to the present and acceptance form part of this change process, and while they might have some similarities with Buddhist practice, this is not overtly intentional.[29]

SCIENTIFIC EVALUATION OF MINDFULNESS THERAPIES

These therapies have been tested and found to show a range of benefits in healthy people as well as people with chronic physical illness and those with a mental illness. But the practice of mindfulness is only one part of three of these therapies, so testing the effectiveness of treatment is not necessarily just a test of whether mindfulness works. It is relatively simple to evaluate mindfulness within each treatment model in isolation, but problems occur when researchers try to lump these therapies together to test whether mindfulness is actually making a difference. This is not good scientific method.

Although there is mounting evidence that mindfulness-based therapies work, there is still a general lack of research studies in this

27 Ost, 'Efficacy of the third wave of behavioural therapies'.
28 Hayes et al., 'Acceptance and commitment therapy'.
29 Harris, *The Happiness Trap*, pp. 164–67.

area. The research that has been conducted has been criticised due to an absence of control comparison groups and a lack of randomisation of participants to treatment groups.[30] This suggests a strong need for better-designed treatment trials to investigate whether mindfulness-based interventions produce change.

Most studies are cross-sectional. They compare different groups of people, for example, people who have used mindfulness and those who have not. But the comparison groups in these cross-sectional studies often do not adequately match participant group characteristics such as age, sociocultural background or lifestyle,[31] and this leaves the studies open to the influence of confounders[32] that might in and of themselves explain why there was a difference between the two groups. The difference might not have been related to the use of mindfulness.

Another research approach is to measure changes within one group of people before and after practising mindfulness, but few studies have followed the same research participants over time to measure the long-term change these mindfulness-based treatments cause.

These scientific methodological problems are more of an issue when we look at research that focuses on the physical benefits and changes in brain function due to mindfulness meditation. This research tends to broadly group meditation and mindfulness together into one construct, and combine more than one therapeutic approach. These studies often do not have a clear working definition of what is being measured, and as we have already seen, mindfulness

---

30 Chiesa & Malinowski, 'Mindfulness-based approaches'.

31 Ibid.

32 A confounding variable is an extra variable that was not accounted for in the experiment. It can influence the results and make them meaningless, as well as introducing bias to findings.

and meditation can mean quite different things in different contexts. It is therefore impossible to accurately calculate what impact this construct has on body and brain functioning.[33]

Nonetheless, the following research investigates the changes in the functioning of the human nervous system (neurophysiology) that have been associated with mindfulness and meditation. In the body, there are two opposing parts of our autonomic nervous system that work together to balance functioning: the sympathetic nervous system, which stimulates our fight or flight response to stress, and the parasympathetic nervous system, which stimulates our rest mode and regulates eating, digestion and sexual arousal. There is building evidence to suggest that meditation increases parasympathetic activity (relaxation) and decreases sympathetic activity (stress). It specifically leads to decreases in heart rate, respiration and systolic blood pressure.[34] These positive physical changes might be one mechanism through which mindfulness and meditation are helpful in reducing the impact of chronic stress.

In the brain, the use of long-term meditation and mindfulness has been linked with improvements in attention, self-control and perception. These changes in mental function have been associated with increased theta activity[35] in the left frontal brain regions, which is interesting because this activity is thought to originate in the anterior cingulate and prefrontal cortex, which are areas associated with emotion processing and sustained attention.[36] Put another way, mindfulness meditation corresponds to increased activation in

---

33 Chiesa & Malinowski, 'Mindfulness-based approaches'.
34 Rubia, 'The neurobiology of meditation'.
35 There are four categories of brain waves – beta, alpha, theta and delta – that range from most active to least active, respectively.
36 Rubia, 'The neurobiology of meditation'.

brain networks of internal attention, and this could trigger activity in regions responsible for positive emotions. In other words, it improves our focus and our mood.

Unfortunately, at this point there are no brain-imaging studies available for either DBT or ACT.[37] Such studies would be helpful. What the few brain-imaging studies do say is that mindfulness and meditation increase emotional control and attention by activating the corresponding brain networks.

A summary of some of the psychological and physical changes that have been associated with mindfulness and meditation are listed in Table 2.1.

EVALUATING MINDFULNESS AS PART OF THERAPY

This short review of the scientific research gives us good reason to be optimistic about the use of mindfulness-based therapy. However, there is still much that is not understood about such therapies.

Psychology is the study of the mind and human behaviour, and the therapies that are developed from it are designed to create healthy change in people. This is a laudable aim. However, it's important that such therapies are established scientifically. A thorough, science-based approach should begin with our understanding of brain function and human behaviour. When this occurs, practice develops based on a hypothesis that can be tested.

To test a hypothesis, we need to clearly define what we mean by mindfulness. It has been defined in a number of different ways depending on the therapeutic approach used: bare attention and lucid

---

37 Chiesa & Malinowski, 'Mindfulness-based approaches'.

Clinical evidence for mindfulness
Improves psychological flexibility and quality of life
Improves emotional regulation
Reduces rumination and worry
Prevents depression relapse
Improves coping with chronic illness
Reduces distress

Neurobiological changes associated with meditation/mindfulness
Decreases heart rate, respiration, blood pressure
Improves attention, self-control, perception and mood
Changes brain activity in networks associated with emotional processing and sustained attention

Table 2.1. A summary of psychological and physical changes associated with mindfulness and meditation

awareness;[38] paying attention to the present moment in a non-judge-mental way;[39] or as a tendency to be aware and mindful in daily life and connected with the present moment.[40] The lack of a consensus about the definition of this term means that it is not clear what we are trying to change. Neither does it allow us to measure this change accurately.

Research suggests that these four mindfulness-based interventions can produce positive change.[41] However, for the main part, proof of whether mindfulness meditation contributes to improving

38 Sun, 'Mindfulness in context', p. 398.
39 Kabat-Zinn, 'Mindfulness-based interventions in context', p. 145.
40 Chiesa & Malinowski, 'Mindfulness-based approaches', p. 406.
41 Ost, 'Efficacy of the third wave of behavioural therapies'.

wellbeing has only been assessed and measured after the therapy has been used, which is a bit like putting the cart before the horse. It has not been theory driven. As we have seen, MBSR is not actually a psychological therapy but a straight Buddhist mindfulness meditation. Both MBCT and DBT are based in a cognitive behavioural approach, but mindfulness meditation has been added in with no scientific foundation.

In comparison, ACT has a more integrated scientific rationale for using mindfulness, and the goal and definition of this practice is slightly different. Connection to the present makes sense when it is informed by and based on functional contextualism, relational frame theory and general cognitive behavioural principles. These theories provide a sound basis for why living in the now is important for psychological wellbeing and how making mindful decisions about events in line with our values contributes to mental flexibility.

Table 2.2 helps us to see some of the contrasts between the worldviews undergirding the Buddhist approach incorporated into MBSR, MBCT and DBT, and that of ACT.

What this discussion really comes down to is what kind of impact we want to have on our life by practising mindfulness. Both Buddhist-based mindfulness and connection to the present moment through mindful living have the common elements of using the five senses, focusing on one thing and developing acceptance and compassion. But they differ quite a lot in other ways.

Buddhism does not acknowledge that people have a self or a soul. This leads on to the concept of interconnection with all living things. Mindfulness is meant to lead to an emptying of the mind and a surrender of desire, which ultimately aims to reduce suffering. The end point is spiritual enlightenment or attainment of insight. In contrast,

Buddhist mindfulness meditation	Mindful connection to the present (ACT)
No self	Self-focus
Use of five senses	Use of five senses
Focus on one thing	Focus on one thing
Acceptance/compassion	Acceptance/self-compassion
Emptying mind	Awareness of mind
Interconnection	Connection to our external and inner world
Surrender of desire	Willingness to change
Influence: Buddhism	Influences: functional contextualism, relational frame theory, cognitive behavioural therapy
Aim: spiritual enlightenment	Aim: psychological flexibility
Value: reducing suffering in the world	Value: living a meaningful life

Table 2.2. Comparison of worldviews undergirding Buddhist mindfulness and ACT

ACT uses self-focus and connection to the self to develop deeper insight into what we think, feel and do. The end point is to develop psychological flexibility so that we do not automatically react unthinkingly to our thoughts, feelings and memories, but become aware of these internal events and take conscious steps to behave in a way that is consistent with creating a meaningful life based on our values.

Put another way, the therapies that have incorporated Buddhist mindfulness are aimed at superficially reducing stress and distress, and creating an inner peacefulness. Acceptance and commitment therapy cuts across this by using our personal values to drive the kind of person we are willing to change into. Mindful connection to the present is just one way of tuning into our internal world so that we become more aware of what we are thinking and feeling, and to learn a new way to interact with these things so that our life is as healthy as possible.

WHERE TO FROM HERE?

As we have seen, a number of modern therapies contain mindfulness and meditative practices, and there is evidence that these therapies improve psychological and physical health. They change our thought patterns, our body's stress response and the brain networks associated with attention and mood.[42] Of the four different therapies discussed, three have openly combined aspects of therapy with Eastern Buddhist religious practices.

It is therefore important for therapists and clients to understand the basis of mindfulness-based interventions and critically consider whether they are compatible and consistent with faith beliefs. Mindfulness-based interventions often do not take into account or show respect for other faith practices because they do not openly acknowledge where these practices come from, or consider that they might be undermining or contradicting the faith practice of people who have a different belief system. For many people who are Jewish, Christian or Muslim, adopting a practice that is Buddhist contravenes their faith. At the least, therapists need to explain what they are teaching and why, so that their clients can make an informed decision. It should not be automatically assumed that clients will willingly engage in this practice. As we considered in the previous

---

42 Moore & Malinowski, 'Meditation, mindfulness and cognitive flexibility'; van der Veldenet al., 'A systematic review'.

chapter, adoption of Buddhist practice may lead people down the path of unhealthy syncretism.

The good news is that we don't have to rely on Buddhist-derived therapies in order to reap the benefits of a mindfulness approach. Acceptance and commitment therapy provides us with a form of mindful connection that is not based on religious tradition or ideology. It is designed to help people move towards greater psychological health through acceptance of painful thoughts and feelings, and its methods are grounded in a clearer scientific framework.

For people like myself who suffer chronic and debilitating pain, life can be very tough. Letting the thoughts, feelings and physical sensations that go with this pain fill our heads and determine our behaviour quickly leads down a path of avoiding any activity that causes or reinforces the pain, and we can be tempted to use anything available to us to limit or obliterate the suffering we are feeling. Mindful living and connection to our experience in the present moment has the power to foster in us greater awareness of these thoughts, feelings and sensations. It encourages us to accept the pain and move to the next step of making choices that are not aimed at avoidance, but instead line up with our values, who we want to be and what kind of life we actually want to live. This is a radical shift in thinking. It means the acceptance of suffering and ending the struggle to manage our distress. The result is a healthier life that is filled with purpose. It is one we want to live.

Of course, this does not mean that everything about ACT is neutral and automatically compatible with the Christian faith. Like any framework, it too should be measured against the Christian worldview to see how compatible it is.

That's where we are headed next.

3

Connecting to the Present, Connecting with God

Connecting to the present changes our approach to life. We will no longer be thinking about the past or worrying about the future. We have no power to change the past and the future has not come yet, but we do have total control over what we choose in the moment. The little, present-focused decisions and actions that are connected to our values accumulate, and it is these that drive the direction our life takes and what kind of person we are. Acceptance and commitment therapy helps us to stay focused on what is important rather than letting our mind take us off on an unhelpful journey of distorted thinking and avoidance of pain.

As followers of Christ, connecting to the present means that we actively choose to be open to our experience of life as it happens. It means embracing suffering as part of living a full life. We are alert, focused, plugged in and using all five senses to connect to our surroundings. It is in this open space of acceptance that we connect to both God and our self.

Yet for so many of us in our frantic, fast-paced culture, we have forgotten what it means to be connected with the present moment. Our attention tends to be splintered by the overload of information streamed to us from various electronic devices throughout our day. This new shattered and shortened attention span is also working change in our brain. It has been suggested that meditation disappeared in Western society with the rise of reason and rational thinking;[1] perhaps the renewed interest in mindfulness is a reactive attempt to pull us back into a more balanced approach to life. It is a desperate grasp for silence, retreat and rest from our overstimulating environment.

We now understand that the brain is a dynamic organ that can heal and alter its functioning by creating new connections between cells. This idea has been popularised by the publication of Norman Doidge's book, *The Brain That Changes Itself*.[2] He presents cases where the practising of new skills has produced alternative neural pathways, which have recovered and improved brain functioning. For example, a stroke survivor can regain movement and function in a part of their body where it was once lost. The same principle applies equally to other brain-related problems such as mental illness. Therapy and counselling provide one means of healing by encouraging changes in thinking and behaviour that in turn create new, healthier connections in the brain.

Mindfulness has been integrated into therapy and treatment to decrease distress and increase wellbeing through sustained attention and focus on the present moment. This assumes not only a change in behaviour because a new skill is being practised, but also a corresponding change in the way our brain functions. The more we practise these techniques, the better we become at them and the stronger the neural pathways for these skills are forged in our brain. Essentially, we are changing our thoughts, feelings and behaviours through repetition.

---

1 Rohr, *The Naked Now*, pp. 109–11.
2 Doidge, *The Brain That Changes Itself*.

Mindful connection to the present as a component of therapy can be assumed to work in a similar way. When we practise this skill, it changes the way our mind works. Equally, if we choose to spend our time engaged in a destructive habit, this will change us too, usually to our detriment, because our effort is being focused on building unhealthy pathways that will inevitably have some manifestation in our life that is negative. Sometimes this can contribute to mental illness.

We tend to be prone to building these unhealthy pathways when we face a problem in life. If we face a worry, a fear, a big life change or a disappointment or loss, our mind takes us to another place. We lose touch with what is happening around us, what people are saying to us, what we are doing physically and what our sensory world is telling us. All we think about is The Problem. It fills up our mind. We all do this with the small things sometimes, like when we are driving our car to work and we can't remember whether the traffic light we just went through was green or red. But with more significant issues, like the death of a family member, this becomes a much bigger problem. No matter what we try, our thoughts, feelings and memories keep focusing on the loss of that person and the pain we feel. It can consume our existence for most of the day, and it can become ongoing. We are actually disconnected to the now.

To numb the pain and anxiety and stress we feel, we can then resort to using a huge variety of distractions to avoid our thoughts and emotions. We drink and eat, take medication, spend money, sleep too much, surf the internet, work more and harder and look at our smart phones. All of these things serve to avoid suffering and are underpinned by an attitude of rejecting our current experience.

But Jesus provides a great example of handling these things in another way. He took time out to be silent, rest, pray and connect to

God and self. He often retreated to a quiet place by himself, especially after spending a lot of time ministering to crowds of people. He accepted life as it was and was compassionate to people. He cried when one of his best friends died. He was open to suffering and did not worry about the problems around him as he had faith that God would provide. In all that he did, he had a continuous connection to God that informed his thoughts and actions. This is an example of living in the present moment.

In this chapter, we compare and contrast the core concepts of ACT with some central elements of Christian thinking in order to explore the similarities between techniques based in therapy versus faith tradition.[3] By investigating this treatment approach more fully, we can explore how some of the concepts and techniques used in ACT can be integrated into our lives to maintain mental health without contradicting our faith.

PSYCHOLOGICAL HEALTH THROUGH CONNECTION WITH THE PRESENT

Acceptance and commitment therapy encourages a change in approach to life. It aims to foster mental flexibility and vital living through engaging in mindful behaviour, accepting unwanted thoughts and feelings, and using values to guide our decisions and actions.[4] All of these components work together to achieve an approach to life that is both resilient and malleable in the face of challenges.

---

3 Acceptance and commitment therapy has been chosen for this dialogue because it is the only psychological therapy reviewed that is based in science and has been shown to be an effective treatment for a range of issues, and which has not adopted Buddhist mindfulness and meditation practices as its framework.

4 Forsyth & Eifert, *The Mindfulness and Acceptance Workbook for Anxiety*; Harris, *The Happiness Trap*; Harris, *The Reality Slap*; Harris & Aisbett, *The Happiness Trap Pocketbook*; Morton & Shaw, *Wise Choices*; Strosahl & Robinson, *The Mindfulness and Acceptance Workbook for Depression*.

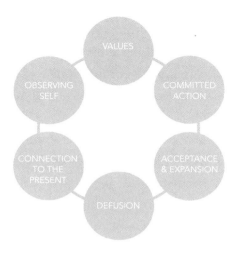

Figure 3.1. Core components of acceptance and commitment therapy

The core concepts of ACT are represented in the diagram in Figure 3.1. They include identifying our values and taking committed action to live according to them. We can learn to make peace with our thoughts and not let them define us, and we can accept painful feelings and use expansion to help us connect back into the present moment through using our observing self, which is the quiet part of our mind. All these things work together to build an approach to life that embraces and accepts our experience in all its different forms

Values

Values define who we want to be and what kind of life we want to live. They are not goals. They focus on being rather than doing. When a number of values are combined, they provide the foundation and motivation to live a full and meaningful life. The choice of what is important to us will flow into decisions we make about who we want to be and what kind of life we want to live. They cover all facets of our life: relationships, spirituality, education and work, relaxation and health.

In ACT, a person's worldview will ultimately determine their values. Their worldview includes their belief system, their culture, the shape of their society and how they think and feel about things. These will be informed further by individualistic values that are specific to that person. A person might have broad values for things like relationships but very specific values in areas such as work or health. Although many of us acknowledge that we hold certain values, very few of us live a life that is totally consistent with them. We often miss the bullseye and manage to live closer to some values than others.

Problems occur when we are living out of sync with our values. In ACT, behavioural change is motivated by the choice to live consistently with the values we name and identify as important to us. The intention is to help us be clear about our values and avoid being sidetracked by unhelpful patterns of thinking, emotions or physical sensations, which can distract us and throw us off course.

Committed action

Acceptance and commitment therapy sees that naming our values is not enough; we also need to commit to acting on them. This is viewed as an issue of the will – that is, we can choose the type of person we want to be and how we are going to live. To live a life that is consistent with our values requires commitment and perseverance.

Acceptance and expansion

In this therapy, the concept of acceptance and expansion is about making room for painful or unpleasant feelings and bodily sensations. To live a full life is to experience the whole spectrum of emotions and physical sensations together with their corresponding thoughts. They are not to be shunned but instead accepted as part of living. Happiness is not the goal; rather, a meaningful life is.

This approach to life flies in the face of many of our Western ideals surrounding the need for happiness and the elimination of suffering. It forces us to question what we want our life to be about and whether happiness really equates to a full life. This is because suffering is a part of our regular experience and comes in many forms, from physical pain and illness to grief and loss and painful inner experiences like sadness, fear, loneliness, shame, regret, guilt and worry.

Acceptance is important because we have limited control over some aspects of life. Working out which things we have the power to change, and which things we cannot, helps us direct our energy to make maximum impact. For those things we cannot change, we can decide to stop the struggle and let go of these problems. For things we can change, we must decide what action to take.

Defusion

The concept of defusion from thoughts is similar to acceptance and expansion. This technique teaches us to accept thoughts and not let them determine our beliefs, feelings and behaviours.

Our thoughts are based in memories and events that have happened in our life and shaped the way we are. Sometimes these thoughts can hook us in and distract us from the present. When this happens we are fusing with them, and this can often be distressing and cause depression or worry. For example, if as a little child at school someone has been humiliated in front of their class because they could not read well, they might have a transcript in their mind that regularly replays whenever they need to read something out loud that says, 'you're such a failure at this.' They might fully believe this thought, which will stop them reading out loud. Defusion teaches a means of accepting these thoughts and making peace with them so that they do not determine beliefs, feelings and actions. In this way, what happened in the past does not have to determine the present.

Defusion can help us to plug back into the here and now and not live a life that is dictated by painful and unhealthy thoughts and feelings. In ACT, this skill is learned through connecting with thoughts and feelings in the present moment using imagination, visualisation and the five senses.

Connection

Connection to our daily experience and living in the present is how we choose to tread the middle road between the past and the future. It allows us to be fully present so we can make healthy choices based on the values that underpin our lives. We need to make a conscious choice and be willing to act in a way that is valued by us.

We are often drawn away by our rational mind and lack the ability to connect. Our rational mind is the constant chatter of our thoughts inside our heads, which has been formed through the varied life experiences we have had. The past impacts our belief about the present. Yet thoughts are necessary; they only become unhealthy and unhelpful when we unquestioningly believe them all to be absolute truth. Mindful connection with the here and now provides us with a sense of distance from these thoughts so we can evaluate them and decide whether they are helpful or unhelpful.

Observing self

Acceptance and commitment therapy uses the concepts of the rational mind and the observing self together. The rational mind is the part of our mind that provides a narrative for our actions and judgements about how we feel. In Western culture this part of our mind dominates our living to the extent that we have lost touch with the observing self. We have valued thinking over other forms of knowledge, and our society has become information saturated. In contrast, the observing self is the part of us that is silent and takes in the present moment through our five senses of touch, taste, smell, sight and sound. This part stays the same and is sometimes referred to as our consciousness. The observing self is vital for connecting with the present and achieving distance from thoughts and feelings so that we can live life to the full in line with our values.

Just as physical exercise builds muscles, the observing self needs to be strengthened through use. It is the part of our mind that we engage during the practice of mindfulness skills. While the goal of mindful connection in ACT is not relaxation, increases in wellbeing nonetheless follow because the strengthening of the observing self builds mental flexibility.

THE CHRISTIAN APPROACH: RENEWING THE MIND

Acceptance and commitment therapy provides a framework for understanding the way people think, feel and behave. Although this framework has come out of CBT, I want to demonstrate that many of its key concepts are consistent with faith in Christ and can be adapted in healthy ways into the way we live. Figure 3.2 presents a comparison of the parallel 'core components' of each worldview, which I'll unpack now.

Christlike values

Acceptance and commitment therapy emphasises the importance of naming our values so that we can live out of them. For the Chris-

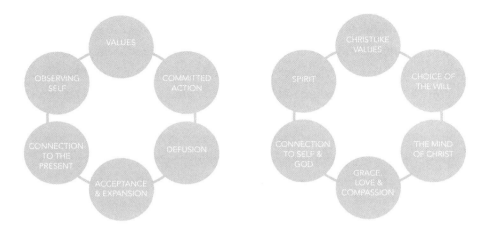

Figure 3.2. Critically contextualising the components of acceptance and commitment therapy with the Christian faith.

tian, we have a clear source for our values. Christ is our example of what it means to be fully human. We see through the account of the Gospels what sort of person he was, living among us as the incarnate God-with-us. He provides us with the teachings of the Sermon on the Mount that outline ethics we can live by (Matthew 5 and 6; Luke 6). He provides the ultimate example of what it means to love God first and love your neighbour as yourself. These are, according to Jesus, the most important things in life (Mt 22:37; Lk 10:27), and they provide a summary of what ought to be the values of Jesus' followers.

If love is central to our experience, this can be taken further by examining Paul's famous passage:

> *Love is patient; love is kind; love is not envious or boastful or arrogant or rude. It does not insist on its own way; it is not irritable or resentful; it does not rejoice in wrongdoing, but rejoices in the truth. It bears all things, believes all things, hopes all things, endures all things. Love never ends' (1 Cor 13:4–8).*

Being a follower of Christ means we will endeavour to live in accordance with these values. Therefore, exploring these values and gauging how consistently we are actually living them out is completely consistent with the approach of ACT. Our values determine what sort of person we want to be, how we relate to other people and how we spend our time. Our Christian values form our foundation; added to these will be other values that are individualistic and consistent with our temperament, natural talents and preferences.

Choice of the will

To choose to follow Christ is a major decision. Faith is both the gift of God and our own decision to actively follow. Jesus warns us that this choice is costly: if we want to follow him, we must deny ourselves and take up our cross. 'For those who want to save their life will lose it, and those who lose their life for my sake will find it' (Mt 16:25). But it is not all about cost; some of it is about will – the decision to let God be in charge of our life.

This is completely contrary to the outlook of our culture in particular, and human nature in general, where we want to live for ourselves.

Therefore, we cannot escape the fact that our will is an important aspect of our life. Just as the will is important for faith, it is an important aspect of ACT because we have to be willing to make change in order to transform our life.

Grace, love and compassion

In the Christian faith, the concepts of grace, love and compassion are the closest to ACT's idea of acceptance and expansion. When we see a friend or family member in pain, we feel compassion for them and want to show that we care, or we might offer to help. To love them is to go a step further and put into practice the values mentioned in 1 Corinthians 13. We will act. Sometimes we just sit with them so they are comforted and know they are not alone. When they make a mistake and are sorry, we might forgive and let the problem go. We might extend this forgiveness when even when the person continues in their behaviour and ignores the hurtful impact it is having on us and other people. These are examples of grace, love and compassion in action.

We are often quick to feel compassion and grace for other people, but we are reluctant and sometimes unable to do the same for ourselves. Neither do we find it easy to accept God's gift of grace to us.

In Ephesians, Paul says,

For it is by Grace you have been saved through faith, and this is not your own doing; it is the gift of God – not by works, so that no one may boast. For we are what he has made us, created in Christ Jesus for good works, which God prepared beforehand to be our way of life (Eph 2:8–10).

And God's grace came through the death and resurrection of Jesus Christ: 'For if the many died through the one man's [Adam's] trespass, much more surely have the grace of God and the free gift [i.e., righteousness] in the grace of the one man, Jesus Christ, abounded for the many' (Rom 5:15).

But instead of freely accepting this gift God has given to us, we struggle with an internal world of difficult feelings: guilt, shame, disappointment, defeat and self-loathing, to name a few. We put ourselves down and think we are stupid, hopeless or a loser. And we replay painful memories that reinforce this over and over in our minds. God's grace extends to us, not just to other people. We need to accept it and make space for these feelings, but not allow them to defeat us. This is an important step that frees us to live life and releases us from our mistakes and disappointments.

Being honest about and accepting our feelings is consistent with what Jesus talked about when he said he came to bring us life to the full (Jn 10:10). To be fully human is to experience all life brings with an attitude of acceptance and openness. It does not mean clinging to old habits and patterns to avoid change, or rejecting and avoiding experiences that are too painful for us. In an imperfect world, suffering will be present. In faith, suffering is a pathway to growth. As Paul says, 'suffering produces endurance, and endurance produces character, and character produces hope, and hope does not disappoint us, because God's love has been poured out into our hearts through the Holy Spirit that has been given to us' (Rom 5:3–5).

The mind of Christ

Paul speaks about cultivating our minds in his letters. In Romans 12:2 he writes, 'Do not conform to the pattern of this world, but be transformed by the renewing of your mind. Then you will be able to test what God's will is – his good, pleasing and perfect will.' And later in 1 Corinthians 2:16 he says that as believers we have the mind of Christ.

The Bible is not a scientific book; these Scriptures guide us to the way, but they don't give us a formula for how this renewing of the mind might be achieved. The renewing of our mind – using techniques such as defusion, acceptance and expansion, and connecting with the present – encourages us to achieve clarity of thought so that we can focus on God's will. These strategies for change do not contradict faith belief. They simply provide a framework to improve our minds.

While this understanding of change is quite individualistic, it does not need to be. It also extends to the transformation and bringing of the kingdom of God in the now.

Connection to self and God

There is nothing specific in Scripture about mindfulness, but there are teachings about how to connect to the present and not be distracted by our thoughts and feelings.

Jesus teaches us not to worry:

Therefore I tell you, do not worry about your life, what you will eat, or about your body, what you will wear. For life is more than food, and the body more than clothing ...

For it is the nations of the world that strive after all these things, and your Father knows that you need them. ...

Do not be afraid, little flock, for it is your Father's good pleasure to give you the kingdom. Sell your possessions, and give alms. Make purses for yourselves that do not wear out, an unfailing treasure in heaven, where no thief comes near and no moth destroys. For where your treasure is, there your heart will be also (Lk 12:22–23; 30; 32–34).

And this is followed up with teaching in 1 Peter: 'Humble yourselves therefore under the mighty hand of God, so that he may exalt you in due time. Cast all your anxiety on him, because he cares for you' (1 Pet 5:6–7).

We are also encouraged not to get caught up in guilt and shame. Instead, we are to confess our sins to God and he will forgive us (1 Jn 1:9), and we are also to confess our sins to each other (Jas 5:16).

Living for the kingdom of God above all things, and putting this kingdom into action in the place where we live, the here and now, is part of praying the Lord's prayer (Lk 11:2). Connection to self and God is something our faith demands of us each and every day. We are to bring every situation to God in prayer and thanksgiving, asking for his help, and he promises to give us peace that 'transcends all understanding' (Phil 4:9). Here, the practice of prayer is part of mindful connection to the present. It extends the type of connection encouraged in ACT, which is more narrowly focused on what is happening in our life. As followers of Christ we are part of something bigger – God's kingdom.

Spirit

Spirit, or soul, is a Christian concept that is comparable to the idea of the observing self that is found in ACT. In Christianity there have traditionally been two types of prayer: mental prayer, and contemplative silent prayer. We are essentially using the quiet part of our self during silent prayer. We will explore this in more detail in Part II.

Now that we have compared ACT with the Christian faith, we can add Christianity to the mindfulness comparison list.

Table 3.1 outlines some of the basic differences between mindfulness practices within Buddhism, secular psychology (ACT) and a style of mindfulness that draws from the Christian mystical tradition.

Overall, there are many aspects of the Christian faith that are entirely consistent with an ACT approach. These include an emphasis on transformation; living according to values; fostering compassion, grace and acceptance; and addressing the issue of the will. Acceptance and commitment therapy assists us towards psychological health by improving our awareness of the observing self and connection with the present moment. It provides tools that help us unhook ourselves from difficult thoughts and accept uncomfortable feelings and bodily sensations. We are free to live in the here and now and fully engage in our life in a meaningful way in line with our faith. This full engagement, based in connection with God and our self, is what I call 'Christ-centred mindfulness'.

Buddhist Mindfulness Meditation	Mindful Connection to the Present (ACT)	Christ-centred Mindfulness
No self	Self-focus	Self and God focus
Use of five senses	Use of five senses	Use of five senses
Focus on one thing	Focus on one thing	Focus on one thing
Acceptance/compassion	Acceptance/ self-compassion	Acceptance/grace
Emptying mind	Awareness of mind	Awareness of mind and God
Interconnection	Connection to our external and inner world	Connection to God and self
Surrender of desire	Willingness to change	Surrender of our will to God
Influence: Buddhist	Influences: functional contextualism, relational frame theory, cognitive behavioural therapy	Influence: Christianity
Aim: spiritual enlightenment	Aim: psychological flexibility	Aim: loving God and the people around us
Value: reducing suffering in the world	Value: living a meaningful life	Value: Christlike spiritual transformation of self and the world

Table 3.1. Comparison of worldviews undergirding Buddhist mindfulness, ACT and Christ-centred mindfulness

WHAT SORT OF CHANGE DO WE REALLY WANT?

In the past century, the church has rediscovered mindfulness techniques that are based on Christian faith and which have been practiced for hundreds of years. They are often referred to as contemplative prayer or Christian meditation. In fact, as we will learn in the next part of the book, it was the work of Brother Lawrence that brought the word mindfulness into the English language with his focus on the continual practice of the presence of God.

Although not proven scientifically, we can assume that Christian-based mindful connection will also reduce stress and distress, focus attention and improve mood, as there is some superficial overlap in technique with Eastern mindfulness meditation practice. The focus on breath, rhythmic speech with a focus on one word, awareness of thoughts and feelings, and the practice of redirecting focus back to the topic of meditation when distractions arise, are all similar. The largest difference between Christian and Buddhist approaches is their underlying worldview, value base and belief system. They differ in their aim, focus and the type of change they are striving for.

The gains made in the last 100 years in understanding the human brain and behaviour can also provide useful tools to facilitate personal change. Acceptance and commitment therapy provides skills of connection to the present moment – defusion, and acceptance and expansion – to assist us in developing self-awareness and free us from unhealthy patterns, so we can live a meaningful life based on our personal values. However, change that is not placed in the context of a value system is a practice without purpose. It will be ultimately unfulfilling.

The danger of mindfulness practices is that they feed into the Western values of individualism and consumerism, which taken to their extreme are narcissistic and empty. Humans were not created to live in isolation or to focus purely on their own needs and desires. This approach leads to emptiness, apathy, self-destruction and lovelessness.

We therefore need to ask ourselves, what sort of change do we want to achieve? Which value system do we want to deepen our connection to?

For the Christian, the resurrection brings with it the power of transformation and change. Paul says we are a new creation; the old life has gone and the new has come (2 Cor 5:17). The mystery of the process is that the Spirit of God works in us and through us to transform our lives so that little by little we become more Christlike. If Jesus is the ultimate model of perfect humanity, we are on the journey of becoming like him in our thoughts, feelings and behaviours.

If we stand back and try to put all of the conversation contained in this section of the book into the scaffolding of Jesus' image of the vine and the branches, we can begin to make sense of where mindful connection to the present fits with contemplative prayer and our faith: being a branch requires connecting to our place in the vine.

There are two parts to this. The first is learning to be mindfully engaged in the present and being prepared to increase our understanding of our self so that we grow and change. The second part of being connected to the vine requires our surrender of will so we are grafted into the vine. It requires relationship between the branch and the vine. This relationship is built on mutual love. On our side, that means learning to love God with a deepening relationship of faith and trust over time. It also means connection with God and the need to practise being present in this relationship, moment to moment, so we are listening to the Spirit's work of creating growth and change in us and in the world. God's part in this process is indwelling us and communing with our spirit to speak truths into our life.

Mindful connection for the follower of Christ is therefore more complex than simple secular practice. It requires surrender of our will and loving God in mutual relationship. It means connecting in the present moment with our self and the world around us, and simultaneously connecting to God every moment of the day. We start to see ourselves and the world around us through God's eyes. It is a different way of seeing. It is to have the mind of Christ.

PART II

Exploring Christian Roots

4

Christ-Centred Mindfulness and the Bible

t the end of the last chapter, we came to see that there is a form of mindfulness that can be Christ-centred. It is founded on the surrender of our will and our love for God. It is centred on both our self and God. And, it uses our mind and our five senses to focus on one thing with the quiet observing part of our mind, which we can refer to as our spirit. Its goal is to transform us by the renewing of our minds so that we might become more Christlike, enabled to love God wholeheartedly and our neighbour as ourselves. This renewal of the mind can occur through connecting with God and self in the present moment, surrendering the will and allowing the work of the Holy Spirit within us.

While we've already looked at some aspects of Christian faith in relation to ACT, it's helpful to spend a bit more time in the Bible to see how the idea of Christ-centred mindfulness fits with the witness of Scripture. It first occurs in the form of meditation on Scripture, or the law as it is called in the Old Testament, and is central to the development of the identity of God's people in the Old Testament. In the New Testament, Jesus adds to this with his teaching on the Spirit and introduces the idea of abiding, using the image of the vine and branches. Post-resurrection, there is a new understanding of mindful connection to God that further emphasises the work of God's Spirit to renew our mind and make us a new creation.

This chapter looks at some of the most prominent themes in the Bible which have informed Christian contemplative practice over the centuries and which we can continue to draw on today.

MEDITATION IN THE OLD TESTAMENT

Meditation has been present from the start of Judaism. After the death of Moses, Joshua became the leader of the Israelites. God gave him specific instructions to cross the Jordan River and take possession of the land on the other side for his people. These were words that God spoke to him.

> *Only be strong and very courageous, being careful to act in accordance with all the law that my servant Moses commanded you; do not turn from it to the right hand or to the left, so that you may be successful wherever you go. This book of the law shall not depart out of your mouth; you shall meditate on it day and night, so that you may be careful to act in accordance with all that is written in it. For then you shall make your way prosperous, and then you shall be successful. I hereby command you: Be strong and courageous; do not be frightened or dismayed, for the LORD your God is with you wherever you go (Joshua 1:7–9).*

This passage is emphasising that the important thing in life is to obey God's divine law as written in the Torah. The law provides the form and shape of faith. It is a means of building a healthy community and living within the order of the created universe. This law is not meant to be a burden. It is a gift.[1] But the instruction is deeper than a command because the words of the law are to be always on

---

1 Butler, *Word Biblical Commentary Joshua 1–12*, pp. 218–21.

the people's lips. They are to meditate on it day and night, and follow it closely in their thoughts and behaviour.

The word translated 'meditate' is important. In Hebrew it means to make a sound, but the form of this sound is non-specific.[2] It can mean making inarticulate sounds, or giving praise to Yahweh. Here in Joshua 1:8, it is thought to refer to a person reading aloud quietly to themself, to study the words and think about the Torah, while maintaining a focus on God.[3] These life-giving laws were meant to liberate the oppressed, provide justice for the weak and establish an egalitarian society. By meditating on them, the Israelites were taking this teaching and making it a deep part of themselves, thinking about it constantly, individually and collectively. It is similar to living mindfully and being aware of God. It is meant to be a seamless part of life.

This is reflected in the way the Psalms are written. We see common themes of reliance on God, meditation on the law (Ps 1), right living, loving God (Ps 48:9), considering all the things God has done (Ps 77:12), God's promises (Ps 119:148), and having an expectation that God will watch over the life of a righteous person. For example, in Psalm 1:2 the Hebrew word that has been translated as 'meditate' means more than just this; it implies some sort of utterance or whispering.[4] This psalm repeats the theme of living for God and living according to the life-giving law, like a tree planted by streams of water.

Happy are those
who do not follow the advice of the wicked,
or take the path that sinners tread,
or sit in the seat of scoffers;
but their delight is in the law of the LORD,

---

2 Ibid.
3 Ibid.
4 Craigie, *Word Biblical Commentary Psalms 1–50*, p. 58.

and on his law they meditate day and night.
They are like trees
planted by streams of water,
which yield their fruit in its season,
and their leaves do not wither.
In all that they do, they prosper.

The wicked are not so,
but are like chaff that the wind drives away.
Therefore the wicked will not stand in the judgement,
nor sinners in the congregation of the righteous;
for the LORD watches over the way of the righteous,
but the way of the wicked will perish (Ps 1).

We see a common theme that forms the foundation of the Israelite identity and faith and daily life. The Israelites are God's people because they are defined by a living and dynamic law that forms righteousness within them and deeply connects them to God.

PRAYER IN THE NEW TESTAMENT

As Messiah, Jesus brings with him the new covenant between God and humanity. He teaches a new way of the kingdom of God and leads us through both example and teaching. We see in his life and ministry that withdrawing from people and spending time alone with God in prayer is necessary and important (Lk 5:15–16). He is essentially continuing the Judaic practice of meditating on God's law and spending time conversing with God silently. His example and teaching in the Gospels takes this further, expanding our understanding of what it means to be in relationship with God and to love him and other people. This is the essence of the kingdom of God he talked about.

Jesus' interaction with Mary and Martha has been used in church tradition to challenge us about the attitude we need to bring to prayer

(Lk 10:38–42). This passage comes at the beginning of the section in Luke's Gospel that contains most of Jesus' teaching on prayer. In this narrative, Mary chose to go against what was expected of her as a woman in her culture. She did not disappear into the kitchen to prepare food for her visitor; instead, she chose to be countercultural and sit with an attitude of love at Jesus' feet and listen to what he was saying.[5] Her posture while she did this shows her respect for Jesus as her teacher as well as her eagerness to learn.

In contrast, Martha offered Jesus hospitality but became distracted by all the work she needed to do because of her invitation. When she realised that Mary did not intend to help her, she became upset and worried. Jesus' rebuke to Martha is important:

> But Martha was distracted by her many tasks; so she came to him and asked, 'Lord, do you not care that my sister has left me to do all the work by myself? Tell her then to help me.' But the Lord answered her, 'Martha, Martha, you are worried and distracted by many things; there is need of only one thing. Mary has chosen the better part, which will not be taken away from her' (Lk 10:40–42).

What this story teaches us is that serving God is fine, as are all the other necessary and mundane aspects of our lives that we do to love and care for other people, but ultimately it is also important to spend time at Jesus' feet, listening, learning and being in relationship. This passage is not saying that contemplation is more important than serving.[6] It is saying that you cannot do one without the other. Just as Mary needed to choose to be countercultural to do this, the challenge for us in our contemporary society is to take time out, be still and silent and spend time with God. This is a lifestyle choice, to limit the constant bombardment of the internet, our mobile phones, the

---

5 Nolland, *Word Biblical Commentary Luke 9:21–18:34*, p. 606.
6 Ibid.

TV and the general fast pace of our busy lives and just sit and be still. We need to work to restore our focus on God. That is all that matters. From this central point of love for God, our love for others will follow. God will also provide clarity about how we spend the remainder of our time.

The parable of the sower is another story that speaks about our attitude to life and listening to God (Lk 8:4–15). Here Jesus uses the image of a farmer scattering seed. From a Jewish perspective, this image of sowing connects to the idea of God giving life and giving the law that needs to bear fruit.[7] The seed falls on four types of ground: on a path, on rock, among thorns and on good soil. Jesus says:

> *Now the parable is this: The seed is the word of God. The ones on the path are those who have heard; then the devil comes and takes away the word from their hearts, so that they may not believe and be saved. The ones on the rock are those who, when they hear the word, receive it with joy. But these have no root; they believe only for a while and in a time of testing fall away. As for what fell among the thorns, these are the ones who hear; but as they go on their way, they are choked by the cares and riches and pleasures of life, and their fruit does not mature. But as for that in the good soil, these are the ones who, when they hear the word, hold it fast in an honest and good heart, and bear fruit with patient endurance (Lk 8:11–15).*

Jesus is challenging us to think about which type of soil we are. We cannot be part of this new life he has come to offer us if we only listen superficially and do not root ourselves in a relationship with God. Neither will we grow and produce fruit based on his teaching if we become distracted by our internal worries and thoughts or by the problems of the external world around us. He is saying that, in order to produce a crop in good soil, we have to listen and persevere.

---

7 Nolland, *Word Biblical Commentary Luke 1–9:20*, p. 373.

It is an intentional choice that takes effort, work and focus. It means paying attention to how we live each moment, and applying God's word to our lives.

Jesus teaches that it is not the length of our verbal or mental prayers that is important (Mt 6:5–8). Neither is he impressed by our outward appearance or how we appear to other people (Lk 18:9–14). This is a strange teaching for those of us who live in a Western, rational culture. God does not just value all our thoughts, feelings, opinions, personal experiences, needs or requests for ourselves or other people. This teaching is more about wanting to spend time with God out of love and enjoy being in God's presence.

> *And whenever you pray, do not be like the hypocrites; for they love to stand and pray in the synagogues and at the street corners, so that they may be seen by others. Truly I tell you, they have received their reward. But whenever you pray, go into your room and shut the door and pray to your Father who is in secret; and your Father who sees in secret will reward you.*
>
> *When you are praying, do not heap up empty phrases as the Gentiles do; for they think that they will be heard because of their many words. Do not be like them, for your Father knows what you need before you ask him (Mt 6:5–8).*

Jesus says, take time out by yourself to spend time with God. Prayer is to be directed at God; it must be genuine and not for display.[8] It is not the amount of time or words we use that is important. God our Father already knows what we need before we ask.

Jesus' disciples asked him to show them how to pray. The example he gives them – what we now know as the Lord's Prayer – is a simple expression of the Jewish prayers of the time. It is distinguished by its simple and direct address to God as our Father, and the confidence that God will answer the requests of his children. It honours God's

---

8 Hagner, *Word Biblical Commentary Matthew 1–13*, p. 142.

name and looks to the coming of God's kingdom. In Matthew, this is extended to say, 'Your kingdom come. Your will be done, on earth as it is in heaven' (Mt 6:10). The remainder of the prayer focuses on addressing our physical and spiritual needs, represented in asking for bread and forgiveness. Matthew 6:12 uses the word 'debts' to refer to a Jewish understanding of moral and religious failures, whereas in Luke 11:4 the word 'sin' is used because it is more relevant in a Greek context.[9] This forgiveness is not just for us, but is given to those who have wronged us. The last part of this prayer identifies our frailty in living according to God's way.

> *He was praying in a certain place, and after he had finished, one of his disciples said to him, 'Lord, teach us to pray, as John taught his disciples.' He said to them, 'When you pray, say:*
>
> *Father, hallowed be your name.*
> *Your kingdom come.*
> *Give us each day our daily bread.*
> *And forgive us our sins,*
> *for we ourselves forgive everyone indebted to us.*
> *And do not bring us to the time of trial' (Lk 11:2–4).*

Reflecting on Jesus' example, we might be tempted to follow this prayer in a formulaic way. This is not what he is teaching. His prayer speaks to our relationship with God and the ushering in of God's kingdom on earth. It is not a kingdom of judgement, violence or control, but of change that starts the moment we begin to follow and give our lives to him. God is interested in us and our physical and spiritual needs, both as individuals and as a collective. This is a radical prayer of transformation.

---

9 Nolland, *Word Biblical Commentary Luke 9:21–18:34*, p. 620.

SURRENDER OF THE WILL

Jesus teaches that to follow the way of God's kingdom and become his disciple requires sacrifice. To follow means to give up our lives and ourselves completely. This is a difficult teaching, and one that we in the West tend to overlook in our faith. Christian faith often becomes a product we consume for our own end, which is not what God wants from us. Both Jesus' teaching and the Christian contemplative tradition emphasise the need to give up all we have: our life, our will and our self.

> *Whoever comes to me and does not hate father and mother, wife and children, brothers and sisters, yes, and even life itself, cannot be my disciple. Whoever does not carry the cross and follow me cannot be my disciple. For which of you, intending to build a tower, does not first sit down and estimate the cost, to see whether he has enough to complete it? Otherwise, when he has laid a foundation and is not able to finish, all who see it will begin to ridicule him, saying, 'This fellow began to build and was not able to finish.' Or what king, going out to wage war against another king, will not sit down first and consider whether he is able with ten thousand to oppose the one who comes against him with twenty thousand? If he cannot, then, while the other is still far away, he sends a delegation and asks for the terms of peace. So therefore, none of you can become my disciple if you do not give up all your possessions (Lk 14:26–33).*

In this passage, the word 'hate' is thought to mean to love less than God. So, to be a follower or disciple of Christ means to love our family less than God.[10] We must be prepared to sell our possessions and not be constrained and shackled to what we own. We need to be willing to suffer as Jesus did. Jesus says, 'No one who puts a hand to the plough and looks back is fit for the kingdom of God' (Lk 9:62).

---

10 Nolland, *Word Biblical Commentary Luke 9:21–18:34*, p. 764.

This is a challenging message that speaks to us about the necessity of giving up our will and starting a new life without looking back.

The contradiction is that in giving up our life to God, we actually begin to find our true selves. Surely, in our modern society of self-centred individualism, this teaching is both a stumbling block and a key to our freedom. A life that only looks to our own needs and desires is empty and destructive because there is no foundation or values to guide it. Yet to let go means giving up our own control and those same desires. A life given over to God is selfless. Prayer that comes from a surrendered life alters the way that we relate to God and the people around us.

ABIDING IN LOVE

For followers of Christ, the selfless life is related to a life of love, the two main components of which are to love God with our heart, soul and mind, and to love our neighbour as our self (Mt 22:36–40). Jesus said these two things sum up the law of the old covenant. A life of love is the fulfilment of the law. These commandments cover the vertical relationship between our self and God, and our horizontal relationship with other people.[11] To live this way is both the inward core and outward sign of the life of a disciple and follower of Christ.

This life of love is guided by the Spirit, who is called Counsellor (or Advocate) and Spirit of truth. John uses the word Paraclete for the Spirit of truth, which we know as the Holy Spirit. The truth is the revelation of God in Christ, and the Spirit of truth therefore brings this revelation to the community of followers.[12]

---

11 Hagner, *Word Biblical Commentary Matthew 14–28*, pp. 643–48.
12 Kysar, *Augsburg Commentary on the New Testament John*, pp. 226–30.

If you love me, you will keep my commandments. And I will ask the Father, and he will give you another Advocate, to be with you for ever. This is the Spirit of truth ...

On that day you will know that I am in my Father, and you in me, and I in you. They who have my commandments and keep them are those who love me; and those who love me will be loved by my Father, and I will love them and reveal myself to them' (Jn 14:15–21).

The Spirit lives, or dwells, in us, which reveals an intimate relationship between the believer and God.[13] Just as Christ lives in relationship with God, so we, through love shown by our obedience, can live in relationship with God the Father, Son and Spirit.[14]

In John 14:26, Jesus repeats his message, saying, 'But the Advocate, The Holy Spirit, whom the Father will send in my name, will teach you everything and remind you of all that I have said to you.' Here the role of the Spirit is to teach the believers and help them to be mindful of what Jesus taught.[15]

Jesus is tying several things together. We show our love for him through choosing to live a life consistent with his teachings and example. The Spirit lives in us and helps us to do this. The mystery is the transformation due to the Spirit's presence in our lives, as well as our awareness of the Spirit's work of change and direction in our thoughts and feelings and behaviour.

This process is best illustrated by Jesus' parable about the vine and the branches.

I am the true vine, and my Father is the vine-grower. He removes every branch in me that bears no fruit. Every branch that bears fruit he prunes to make it bear more fruit. You have already been cleansed by the word that I have spoken to you. Abide in me as I abide in you. Just as the branch cannot

---

13 Ibid.
14 Ibid., p. 232.
15 Ibid.

bear fruit by itself unless it abides in the vine, neither can you unless you abide in me. I am the vine, you are the branches. Those who abide in me and I in them bear much fruit, because apart from me you can do nothing. Whoever does not abide in me is thrown away like a branch and withers; such branches are gathered, thrown into the fire, and burned. If you abide in me, and my words abide in you, ask for whatever you wish, and it will be done for you. My Father is glorified by this, that you bear much fruit and become my disciples. As the Father has loved me, so I have loved you; abide in my love. If you keep my commandments, you will abide in my love, just as I have kept my Father's commandments and abide in his love. I have said these things to you so that my joy may be in you, and that your joy may be complete.

This is my commandment, that you love one another as I have loved you. No one has greater love than this, to lay down one's life for one's friends. You are my friends if you do what I command you. I do not call you servants any longer, because the servant does not know what the master is doing; but I have called you friends, because I have made known to you everything that I have heard from my Father. You did not choose me but I chose you. And I appointed you to go and bear fruit, fruit that will last, so that the Father will give you whatever you ask him in my name. I am giving you these commands so that you may love one another (Jn 15:1–14).

In Jesus' culture, the image of a grapevine was a tangible way to explain the process of what the Spirit does. By the teachings John outlines in chapter 14, remaining in the vine, which represents Christ, means loving God and following Jesus' teachings.[16] It means 'abiding in' or being bound together with Christ – to have faith and trust in him.[17]

When we do this, our thoughts, feelings and behaviours that are contrary to his way are pruned off. The other side to this relationship is that Jesus calls us to bear fruit. Our transformation is God's initia-

---

16 Ibid., p. 238.
17 Ibid.

tive, and it will result in us going out into the world and spreading this transformation to other people and throughout our society.[18]

By necessity, this process develops our self-awareness. But the crunch comes when we realise that in order to produce any fruit we need to be connected to Christ continuously. Each day we need to be mindful of God's presence in all we think, feel and do, in order to change and have healthy and productive lives. These lives are not productive for our own benefit but for God and those around us. This is because our will has been surrendered in the process of being grafted to the vine. The purpose of our lives becomes living for God. There is no divide between living our faith in a practical sense and contemplative prayer. They are all intertwined.

THE HOLY SPIRIT AND BREATH

Connection to God through an abiding relationship centred on love is not adequate in itself. There is a space within this relationship where God communicates with us at a very deep level. This is done through the Holy Spirit.

In Genesis 2:7 we see that God breathed into humankind the breath of life. It is God that gives us life and who is the source of our life. This same idea of God breathing life into us appears in Job 27:3, Job 12:10 and Job 32:8. 'But it is the spirit in man, the breath of the Almighty, that gives him [humankind] understanding' (Job 32:8).

This idea of breath is taken further in light of the resurrection of Christ, in the final third mention of the Paraclete, or Spirit, in John 20. This passage starts at the point where the women go to the tomb and find it empty, and Jesus appears to Mary. Shortly afterwards,

---

18 Ibid., pp. 236–43.

Jesus appears to his disciples in a locked room.

> *When it was evening on that day, the first day of the week, and the doors of the house where the disciples had met were locked for fear of the Jews, Jesus came and stood among them and said, 'Peace be with you.' After he said this, he showed them his hands and his side. Then the disciples rejoiced when they saw the Lord. Jesus said to them again, 'Peace be with you. As the Father has sent me, so I send you.' When he had said this, he breathed on them and said to them, 'Receive the Holy Spirit. If you forgive the sins of any, they are forgiven them; if you retain the sins of any, they are retained' (Jn 20:19–23).*

This image of breathing on the disciples and giving them the Holy Spirit is significant. It further expands on Jesus' teaching on the Spirit in John 14 and 15. Breath in this context is more than life. It is God's Spirit living in us.

A theological understanding of God's Spirit recognises that the Spirit is both the source of life and also the person who links us with God, like a go-between. [19] When we make sense of this in the context of mindful connection to the present moment in relation to self and God, it is more significant. The observing self – our consciousness or the quiet part of our mind – is the place where our spirit communes with God's Spirit. It is here that in the follower of Christ a unique transforming power exists.

Contemplative prayer and mindful connection to God in this context gives a basis for mindful focus on our breath. The breath represents both the life God gives us and the presence of the Holy Spirit in our life. Second to this, mindfully connecting to God allows God to speak truths to us that transform our thoughts, feelings and behaviours. It also deepens our love for, and relationship with, God. The more we foster this mindful awareness and connection to God

---

19 Moltmann, *The Source of Life*; Taylor, *The Go-Between God*.

and our self, the more we are guided by the Spirit in all we do. We begin to listen and see things with a new type of sight.

THE RESURRECTION LIFE

Paul expands this understanding of what it is like to live in the power of the resurrection, the new life that Christ has breathed into us. He calls the Spirit 'the Spirit of life that sets us free' (Rom 8:2). We no longer live by trying to follow a set of laws because the law is now fulfilled out of our love for God and by the power of the Spirit.[20] Paul writes, 'those who live according to the Spirit have their minds set on the things of the Spirit. To set the mind on the flesh is death, but to set the mind on the Spirit is life and peace' (Rom 8:5–6).

In our minds, this type of new way of living means we will be totally transformed and we are on our way to becoming like Christ, the example of what it is to be fully human. In Romans 12 it says, 'Do not be conformed to this world, but be transformed by the renewing of your minds, so that you may discern what is the will of God – what is good and acceptable and perfect' (Rom 12:2). The Spirit works in our observing self, transforming our rational mind – which contains our thoughts, feelings and behaviours – and guiding us and showing us the way to live as Christ. We can listen and hear the direction God wants us to go in our speech and actions.

Paul expands this teaching further in 1 Corinthians 2:6–16. The Spirit gives us wisdom. This is not rational thought; it is deeper and more profound. He writes:

The Spirit searches everything, even the depths of God. For what human being knows what is truly human except the human spirit that is within? So also no one comprehends what is truly God's except the Spirit of God. Now

---

20 Dunn, *Word Biblical Commentary Romans 1–8*, pp. 435–37.

we have received not the spirit of the world, but the Spirit that is from God, so that we may understand the gifts bestowed on us by God. And we speak of these things in words not taught by human wisdom but taught by the Spirit, interpreting spiritual things to those who are spiritual ... But we have the mind of Christ (1 Cor 2:10–13, 16).

The power of the resurrection in the follower of Christ is a deep renewing power in our mind that brings wisdom. This presence within us creates in us the mind of Christ.

Knowing that the process of change is not just our choice and effort is a great comfort and relief. As followers of Christ, this process of surrendering our will to God, living a life of love for God and those around us and staying connected to God each moment of the day means that change is partly our choice and partly God's power working in us through the Spirit. The great difficulty is that, in our present culture, few of us want to embark on the costly road of surrendering our will. To love, we need to spend time building relationships – and this takes effort and commitment, which are scarce commodities in our modern Western culture.

PUTTING THE PARTS OF THE PICTURE TOGETHER

Throughout God's written word we see several themes emerge. There is a deep connection between the concept of meditating and the habit of reflecting on Scripture in all that we do each day so that we can live the life that God intended us to experience in relationship with him.

Jesus extends this teaching by challenging us about our attitude to prayer and listening to what God is saying to us. He came to bring a new kingdom that transforms us personally and as a society. Following this new way requires us to surrender our will and follow Christ. It means loving God and the people around us. It demands a new form of relationship with God where we are bound to him in a mutual relationship that shapes us and enables us to go into the world to act as agents of change.

None of this happens just based on our own effort or choice. God breathes into us his Spirit that guides us at the level of our consciousness – or observing self. The gift of the Holy Spirit challenges our thoughts, feelings and behaviour, as well as bringing power for transformation. This happens because of our abiding relationship with Christ. We have begun a journey to become like him. We have the mind of Christ. Mindful connection to God in this context is powerful and life giving.

5

Christian Mystics Rediscovered

Since the founding of the church, there has been a consistent mystic influence in Christian faith practice, which has result-ed in the development of many and varied forms of medita-tion and contemplative prayer. These practices use the same part of our mind that ACT refers to as our observing self. It is unfortunate that many of these practices are little known today and therefore timely for us to rediscover them to widen and enrich our lives.

Christian meditation and contemplative prayer practices have three main features that distinguish them from other forms of med-itation and mindfulness. The first is the focus, which is on God and not just the self. The second is an issue of the will. The aim of most contemplative practices is to move towards the total surrender of our will and life to God. The third feature is the desire to love God completely in an all-consuming way.

In this chapter we're going to take a look at the key writings of the Christian mystics of the Middle Ages. Of course, many of their prac-tices reach back further than this to the beginning of the early church. For example, the pioneering Antony (AD 251–356) gave up all he had and retreated to a life in the desert, walled up in an unused fort for twenty years and consuming only bread and water.[1] Others like Simeon (390–459), who lived upon a sixty-foot pole on a six-foot square platform for thirty-six years, undertook a more extreme ascetic lifestyle.[2] A third movement practiced solitude with other Christians by forming the first early monastic communities, starting with Pachomius in 323 and followed by others including Basil of Caesarea (329–379), Augustine of Hippo (354–430) and John Cassian (360–435).[3]

But the writings from 1300 to 1600 are a particularly rich source for exploring the diversity of the mystic tradition. Most of the practices we're looking at in this chapter were developed before the rise of Protestantism in the 1500s. They were therefore established and remain better known within the Catholic tradition, but there has been a growing appreciation of them in evangelical circles in more recent years. We will place them within their cultural and historical worldviews in order to get a taste of the diversity and richness of these traditions. At the end of each section, these forms of Christian meditation and contemplation will be compared and contrasted with secular mindfulness.

These texts are quite difficult to read because they use older expression and style, and some of them are lengthy, repetitive and hard to follow. This is not helped by the fact that several of them were originally written in another language, such as Spanish, and have been translated into English. To make them more accessible to the reader, I have summarised their context briefly. If they pique your interest, I encourage you to delve into the full text for yourself.

By rediscovering our Christian tradition of contemplative prayer and meditation, we will discover that there was a type of mind-

---

1 Guy, *Introducing Early Christianity,* p. 143.

2 Ibid, p. 161.

3 Ibid, p. 151.

ful connection that focused on both self and God simultaneously. Learning why these techniques were used to enrich faith will help us understand how they can deepen our connection with God and cultivate spiritual discipline in our life that contributes to wellbeing. The hope is that through this exploration and rediscovery, we will realise just how relevant Christ-centred mindfulness is to everyday life.

THE CLOUD OF UNKNOWING

The Cloud of Unknowing was written in the 1300s and comes from the mystic influence of the Neo-Platonists.[4] Little is known about the identity of the writer other than that he was most probably a cloistered monk, possibly a Carthusian. *The Cloud of Unknowing* was known and read by English Catholics up until the seventeenth century.

The writer of this text speaks about the need to enter a cloud of unknowing, which is a darkness that we enter between ourselves and God, in order to come to a deeper communion. To reach this contemplative state, we need to leave all thoughts and feelings under a cloud of forgetting. The writer speaks about focusing on a word ('God' or 'love') rather than on many thoughts about God. In so doing, we are beating upon the cloud of unknowing.

The writer speaks about the difference between someone called to lead an active Christian life and one called to live the life of contemplation, suggesting that a person cannot live both ways but will spend most of their time in one or the other state. He uses Mary and Martha to illustrate this: Mary sat at Jesus feet out of love to further understand her Lord, whereas Martha was concerned about practical issues. The writer says that the tension that existed between these two women is the same as that which exists between contemplatives

---

4 Unknown, *The Cloud of Unknowing*.

and actives: actives are often complaining about the contemplative's lack of action, but the contemplative needs to graciously accept this criticism and continue to do what they do best.

For those who are troubled by sinful urges and thoughts, the writer says that they need to step above these thoughts, and with a stirring of love step them under their feet. They need to 'cover them with a thick cloud of forgetting.'[5] When the thoughts rise up again, even more effort needs to be put into treading them down again. For people having trouble doing this, he recommends that they try to pretend these thoughts are not there and focus on God. He also suggests asking God for help with thoughts we are not strong enough to fight. He goes on to speak about the pain this struggle causes, but encourages perseverance, because with time the process of warring against these thoughts and feelings becomes lessened, though it persists nonetheless.

The writer discusses the distractions caused by feelings, which also need to be trodden under the cloud of forgetting, and about destroying these feelings through grace, with the effect that it will produce great sorrow. The only feeling in body and spirit that is reliable is found from devout prayer. It is based on love for God and comes in the form of abundant gladness: 'For God will be served with body and with soul both together, as seemly is, and will reward man his merit in bliss, both in body and in soul.'[6] The writer also warns that other strategies to focus inward can lead people to a false knowledge of God's presence as experiences in their body. For some, imagination and pride cause them to adopt strange religious behaviours, and the writer sees these as revealing an unhealthy restlessness of mind and unstable heart.

---

5 Unknown, *The Cloud of Unknowing*, ch. 31.
6 Ibid., ch. 48.

This text needs to be considered from within the culture and period of writing. It creates a dichotomy between the physical and spiritual world, which we often hear referred to as a dualistic theology and worldview. This dualism repeats in the emphasis on the life of the contemplative as different to one of the active Christian, and the contrast between the choices of Mary and Martha. It is therefore not surprising that *The Cloud of Unknowing* separates contemplation from active life and results in a method that attempts to control thoughts and push bodily urges and feelings down and away. The body is seen as inferior to the soul. Towards the end of the text, the writer goes further still and dismisses the value of our physical senses explicitly:

> For by thine eyes thou may not conceive of anything, unless it be by the length and the breadth, the smallness and the greatness, the roundness and the squareness, the farness and the nearness, and the colour of it. And by thine ears, nought but noise or some manner of sound. By thine nose, nought but either stench or savour. And by thy taste, nought but either sour or sweet, salt or fresh, bitter or liking. And by thy feeling, nought but either hot or cold, hard or tender, soft or sharp. And truly, neither hath God nor spiritual things none of these qualities nor quantities. And therefore leave thine outward wits, and work not with them, neither within nor without.[7]

In many ways, *The Cloud of Unknowing* has a vastly different approach to that of popular mindfulness practice and connection with the present. This is partly caused by the different worldviews in which they have been developed. The writer sees the physical body and soul as being distinct parts of our humanity, with the physical body and world not valued as highly as the soul and spiritual world. This results in a type of contemplation that is more meditative in nature.

---

7 Unknown, *The Cloud of Unknowing*, ch. 70.

The influence of the physical world is diminished in favour of focusing on God and our love for him, and attaining a form of spirituality that is uplifting and transformative.

This method of contemplative prayer conflicts with ACT because it advocates a struggle to *control* thoughts and feelings and to block them from the mind. Acceptance and commitment therapy teaches that this strategy is ineffective because the more we struggle to control thoughts, feelings and urges, the greater the intensity with which they reoccur and consume us. It is better to drop the rope in this tug-of-war and accept their presence, then either redirect our focus onto something we are doing or choose to take action in line with our values.

The Cloud of Unknowing overlaps more with mindful connection where the writer focuses on trying to take the emphasis off rational thinking, feelings and urges in order to still the mind. This resembles in part 'the observing self'. However, it moves beyond focusing on the self or physical world to focusing on God.

The main practice that comes from *The Cloud of Unknowing* is the act of attending to one faith-based word for an extended period of time. This form of contemplative prayer can be used to extend our understanding of how our faith relates to the observing self.

TERESA OF AVILA: *INTERIOR CASTLE*

Teresa of Avila was a Carmelite nun who lived in Spain in the 1500s, during the time of the Inquisition.[8] This was a time of great change and religious turmoil. As a mystic and reformer of her Carmelite order, she was at risk of religious persecution. Her writings at the time

---

8 Teresa of Avila, *Interior Castle*.

were vetted by the church and have survived time to remain a classic of Christian literature. St Teresa wrote *Interior Castle* over a period of three months at age sixty-seven.[9] Her intended audience was her fellow nuns, with whom she wished to share some of her insights about prayer and the soul. The work was canonised by the Catholic Church 100 years after her death.

St Teresa had intentions to write a work on prayer, and at the time had been contemplating the soul, when God gave her a vision of a crystal globe made in the shape of a castle. It contained seven mansions; the innermost was the King of Glory, which illuminated the rest of the castle. Outside the castle there was darkness, and an assortment of creatures like snakes and toads. This vision forms the basis of the *Interior Castle*, and in each of the chapters of her book she takes us deeper into this vision of prayer and the soul. The goal is to inspire followers to go deeper into a life of prayer and explore the different facets of it, and in so doing to reach a state of humility and selflessness that is totally abandoned to the will of God. This is not meant to lead to religious inner retreat, but rather to provide a new and different source from which all life activity can be based.

This text has survived through time because it teaches us much about God and ourselves. There are themes in St Teresa's text that are broadly applicable to developing an awareness of our thoughts and emotions and practising mindful connection in the present moment to our self and God.

The first mansion, which symbolises a stage of entering prayer and mediation in order to gain self-knowledge, is comparable to a psychological use of the observing self to gain a better understanding of our thoughts and feelings. St Teresa says we need to delve into

---

9 Ibid.

the soul and understand it in order to progress our faith and personal understanding. She says: 'As to what good qualities there may be in our souls, or Who dwells within them, or how precious they are – those are things which we seldom consider and so we trouble little about carefully preserving the soul's beauty.'[10] We must spend time in introspection to understand ourselves.

She identifies impediments in our lives that are equally relevant today as in the past. These include being in a constant state of activity and weighed down with the problems and distractions of life. As she says,

> There are souls so infirm and so accustomed to busying themselves with outside affairs that nothing can be done for them, and it seems as though they are incapable of entering within themselves at all. So accustomed have they grown to living all the time with the reptiles and creatures to be found in the outer court of the castle that they have become like them.[11]

And again she writes that there are souls who eventually enter the castle of prayer and meditation, but:

> Full of a thousand preoccupations as they are, they pray only a few times per month, and as a rule they are thinking all the time of their preoccupations, for they are very much attached to them, and, where their treasure is, there is their heart also ... Eventually they enter the first rooms on the lowest floor, but so many reptiles get in with them that they are unable to appreciate the beauty of the castle or to find any peace within it. Still, they have done a good deal by entering at all.[12]

This observation highlights our need to connect with the present and become aware of our thoughts, feelings and behaviours. To fail

---

10 Teresa of Avila, *Interior Castle*, p.4.
11 Ibid., p.7.
12 Ibid., p.8.

to do so risks our lives becoming choked by the things around and within us. This is so relevant in the information age where we are constantly bombarded by electronic stimulation and live life at a frenetic pace. Here, Teresa invites us to go against the flow of our society. Developing the observing self through prayer and mindful connection can assist us in this journey, because the regular practice of observing our thoughts and feelings allows us more insight into our inner life, and in gaining this understanding we are better able to change how we respond to them.

In Teresa's conception, self-knowledge is important because it brings humility, and we cannot know ourselves unless we also seek God. This makes sense when we realise that humankind was made in God's image. To know ourselves, we need to know God.[13]

Teresa writes that if we do not understand our own thoughts and feelings, they can distract us from what is important, to the point where their effect is deleterious to us and we feel discouraged and upset. This resonates with the ACT concept of experiential avoidance. Our thoughts and feelings have the capacity to throw our life off track and set us on a path to a life that is inconsistent with our values and beliefs. Moreover, she recognises that the thoughts of our rational mind can interfere with our ability to concentrate while prayerfully contemplating. This can become tedious and discouraging, but it should not put us off this practice.

Teresa's solution to this dilemma is not unlike mindful connection to the present moment. She writes about putting a stop to discursive reasoning and gently redirecting attention to being in God's presence. This type of prayer is consistent with ACT, because each and every time we get distracted by our rational mind, we are to

---

13 Ibid.

gently redirect our attention back to what we are doing. By doing this we are intentionally using our observing self: not trying to block our thoughts, but allowing them to be there and still using the will to direct our attention. The only difference here is that we are mindfully praying instead of mindfully doing some other task. The focus of prayer in this instance is to mindfully focus on God.

Perhaps the most helpful thing we can learn from Teresa's writings is the importance of understanding ourselves. The path to prayer and a deepening understanding of God and our self is a journey that requires awareness and acceptance of our inner thoughts and feelings and a development of the observing self. It requires freely giving up our will in order to have it lost in God's. A progression in this inner understanding and prayer with God in turn changes us so that we become more like him. Rather than retreating further into ourselves, it necessitates a radical change that is apparent in how we serve God in the world and relate to other people.

IGNATIUS OF LOYOLA:
THE SPIRITUAL EXERCISES

St Ignatius was born in a wealthy family in Spain in 1491.[14] He was the youngest of thirteen children and lived in a family that identified themselves as Christian, but who did not live according to the teachings of the faith they professed. Ignatius was raised to serve his country as a courtier and diplomat, and he had a relatively sparse education. In his early life he lived for himself and was a known womaniser. He committed serious crimes, for which he escaped punishment due to his status and position, and went on to serve as a soldier. During a battle, he helped defend the town of Pamplona

---

14 Traub & Mooney, *A Biography of St Ignatius of Loyola*.

against an attack by the French and his leg was shattered by a cannonball. This injury devastated his life, and his recovery was slow and required many weeks in bed. He started reading religious books to pass the time and began to rely on his imagination to keep him occupied. This was a turning point in his life, when for the first time his faith became important to him.

On recovery from his injury, Ignatius went on a pilgrimage with the intention of travelling to Jerusalem.[15] He gave away his fine clothes to the poor, gave up his sword and dagger, and started to transform his life. He got as far as Manresa, and for ten months he worked and would spend many hours per day praying. His notes about the spiritual experiences he undertook formed the basis of what has become known as *The Spiritual Exercises*. These were approved by the Vatican in 1548.[16]

The Spiritual Exercises provide a structure for self-examination. The first week focuses on introspection of our faults as evidenced in thought, speech and behaviour. Three times per day, morning, noon and night, time is set aside to reflect on these things. He provided a structure for these reflections:

1. Give thanks to God.
2. Ask for grace to know what our sins are and to rid ourselves of them.
3. Examine our thoughts, speech and behaviour minute by minute, hour by hour, from the last period we stopped to do this until the present moment.
4. Ask God's forgiveness for things we have done.
5. Ask for God's grace to change.

---

15 Ibid.
16 St Ignatius of Loyola, *The Spiritual Exercises*, p. 256.

The second week of exercises focuses on the life of Christ. Each day there is a series of five contemplations, lasting for one hour each, to be done at midnight, dawn, Mass, Vespers and before supper. The structure of prayer is similar to that of the first week, beginning with giving thanks to God. Then the imagination is used to enter into biblical scenes and to see the synagogues, towns and villages where Jesus taught. We are to focus on God's call and his divine will for our life. In doing this, we bring to mind the image of a human king interacting with his subjects and use that image as a basis of reflection on our relationship with God.

The third week covers the events around Jesus' death. The reflections follow the same pattern of contemplations as the second week, occurring five times throughout the day. In the fifth contemplation of the day, the five senses are again used to fully experience these scenes. The first day starts with giving thanks to God. Then we are encouraged to remember the events around the last supper, including the journey from Bethany to Jerusalem, Jesus washing the disciples' feet and the Last Supper. We are invited to see and hear these places in our imagination, then to feel all the emotions, especially the grief and sadness, that surround the realisation that Jesus is preparing to die on the cross for us. The focus for this week is to fully feel the suffering of Christ and the sadness and grief associated with these events.

The fourth week is focused on the resurrection of Christ and his divinity, and the ability for this to offer us consolation. In this week, the emphasis is on feeling joyful and intentionally thinking about things that bring spiritual happiness. To aid this cause, the environment can be helpful – for example, sitting in the sun and feeling the warmth on our skin, or feeling the wind in our face. Again, fasting is encouraged if it helps maintain focus on these contemplations. We are encouraged to adapt the subject of our contemplations in a similar way to what was practised in the second and third weeks. Instead of doing these exercises five times per day, this is reduced to four: when you wake in the morning, at Mass or before dinner, at Vespers and at supper, when again the five senses are used.

Ignatius provides three methods of contemplative prayer during the fourth week. The first method provides concepts that can be helpful to reflect on in prayer, including the 'Ten Commandments', 'Seven Deadly Sins', 'Three Powers of the Soul' and 'Five Senses'. The goal is to consider each power of the soul, and each of the senses, and imitate Christ in the way we use them. The second method contemplates the meaning of each word in a prayer. In this method a person intentionally focuses on one word, for example, 'Father', for the period of one hour. At the end of this hour the person asks God for what they need, and then the time of contemplation ends. The third method uses the rhythm of breath. While saying words slowly with each breath, the person can think about the meaning of each word, moving through the words of a prayer or focusing on just one or two words over an extended period of time.

Reading St Ignatius' work in its original form is not easy, as his writing is not very ordered and clear. It is a product of his education and the time in which he lived, with a strong emphasis on sin, purgatory, the holiness of Mary and images that reflect the understanding of faith and society at that time – for example, imagining Christ as our king or commander-in-chief. If a reader can persevere with these things and glean the meaning behind his teaching, the relevance of *The Spiritual Exercises* is profound. What St Ignatius was trying to get people to do is examine themselves and their thoughts, feelings and behaviours, and decide what needs to change. He was using the measuring stick of his faith to do this. For Christians of our time, this is still relevant. We can add to this with other psychologically based tools to change unhelpful thoughts and behaviours – for example, by using the strategies of acceptance and expansion and defusion in ACT. This is similar to how St Ignatius used other ideas related to the human condition from his culture, for example, the Seven Deadly Sins.

The ultimate goal of *The Spiritual Exercises* is inner transformation and a Christ-centred life, yet they also aim to increase wellbeing and psychological health. These exercises have many things in common with mindful connection to the present in their use of the breath, the five senses and the imagination, and their cultivation of singular focus and awareness of thoughts and feelings. They rely predominantly on using the observing self to foster internal awareness and are revolutionary in that they consider all aspects of the person's environment – the amount of light, the sun and wind on the skin, food and sleep, and the movement of the body – as part of the exercises.

BROTHER LAWRENCE:
THE PRACTICE OF THE PRESENCE OF GOD

The Practice of the Presence of God was written in the 1600s.[17] It is based on a series of four conversations with, and fifteen letters by, Brother Lawrence, a Carmelite brother who lived in France.

Brother Lawrence was converted to Christianity at age eighteen after reflecting on God's providence and power in bringing the changing of seasons to a tree.[18] In winter the tree was dormant, then

---

17 Brother Lawrence, *The Practice of the Presence of God.*
18 Ibid.

it would become green and grow fruit, and then it would drop its leaves ready for winter. This spiritual revelation inspired him to enter a monastery with the intent to sacrifice his life to God. To his surprise, he found this life to be one of nothing but deep satisfaction. What marked his monastic lifestyle as different was his continual conversation with God, so that there was no essential difference between scheduled prayer time and other periods throughout the day. His contemplative practice was holistic and embedded in all he did and said. He lived with a continual sense of God's presence.

The following passage encapsulates the main tenets of Brother Lawrence's lifestyle and spiritual practice:

> That we should establish ourselves in a sense of GOD's Presence, by continually conversing with Him ... That we ought to give ourselves up to GOD, with regard both to things temporal and spiritual, and seek our satisfaction only in the fulfilling of His will, whether He lead us by suffering or by consolation, for all would be equal to a soul truly resigned.[19]

This passage has important themes of acceptance, the giving up of our will to God and having a continual sense of God's presence. Brother Lawrence introduces a new form of contemplative prayer that could be practiced continuously and during everyday activities. His method essentially does not discriminate between set prayer times and the rest of the day; rather, it is about adopting a particular attitude in all we do.

This spiritual lifestyle is intentional and must be learned with effort at the start, just like learning a new skill, but with time it becomes habit:

---

19 Ibid., First Conversation.

That in order to form a habit of conversing with GOD continually, and referring all we do to Him; we must at first apply to Him with some diligence: but that after a little care we should find His love inwardly excite us to it without any difficulty.[20]

He talks of the problem of having interrupting and wandering thoughts that distract from focusing on God. He commented that we ought to reject them and return our focus to communion with God. He 'considered GOD as the end of all his thoughts and desires, as the mark to which they should tend, and in which they should terminate.'[21]

The way Brother Lawrence speaks about keeping his focus on God and his love for God is similar to having an intentional connection with the present moment. When he finds he has become distracted, he notices his mistake and returns his focus on God.

Brother Lawrence's method of contemplative prayer is very similar to mindfully connecting with the present moment. It requires the will to persevere in its practice, the development of the observing self to focus on the task and a diminished reliance on the distracting rational mind. To maintain this discipline requires the same practice of focusing on one thing, and when distraction occurs, it requires a redirection of attention back to the task at hand. The difference is that in secular mindfulness the focus is on the present moment, and in Brother Lawrence's contemplative method it is on experiencing the continual presence of God.

It is also interesting how thoughts, feelings and physical pain are handled during this form of contemplation. He openly accepts that our mind will distract us from thoughts and points out that allowing these distractions to frustrate us is simply another way we can get

---

20 Ibid., Second Conversation.
21 Ibid., Fourth Conversation.

thrown off task. This is a really important point, because for many people the greatest challenge and deterrent for meditating or praying can be the incessant distractions produced by our rational mind. For someone to acknowledge them as part of the process of learning to focus can be a great relief. The more we practice, the better we become, and we will have days where this is easier than others.

Acceptance of pain and suffering is advocated, and this also does not need to distract from practising the presence of God. Here we find a Christian-based form of mindfulness and acceptance of difficult emotions and physical sensations. Rather than trying to escape them, there is another pathway that allows room for them in our experience so they can teach us more about ourselves and help us to grow as people. This idea is similar to the concepts of expansion, acceptance and connection with the present, which we find in ACT.

Brother Lawrence's practice of the presence of God is almost identical to that of mindful connection to the present using the observing self. It brings an attitude of acceptance and can be practiced throughout our whole day without interruption. Rather than struggling with thoughts and feelings that distract, attention is gently refocused to the present and onto God. The main point of difference between his method and secular mindfulness is the deep underlying significance of his lifestyle. In order to practise the presence of God, his will was completely surrendered to God. Everything he said or did was done out of love for God, and his contemplative prayer was totally God focused, whereas mindfulness is self-focused.

EMBRACING OUR TRADITION

These four mystic traditions teach us that in order to pray and connect with God, we need to have an equally strong awareness of self.

There are several different methods outlined in these approaches: separating our rational mind from our observing self; learning how to focus on God rather than being distracted by worries and memories and other activities around us; abandoning our will to God and choosing an attitude to life that is about learning; and being unafraid to use imagination, our five senses and the physical world to help us in this task.

Contemplative prayer or Christ-centred mindfulness can be practiced alone or while doing mundane tasks. It can be integrated seamlessly into our daily life so that there is no clear distinction between prayer and action; all are focused on a present moment connection to both God and our self.

The essential parts of this approach are to:

1. Focus on one thing.
2. Use our five senses and imagination to do this.
3. Accept that distractions will come.
4. When necessary, simply redirect our focus.
5. Persevere in this discipline.

In Part III of this book, these mystic traditions will be adapted and updated to make them relevant to life in the twenty-first century. A series of practical exercises have been provided so that we can continue to use these approaches in our daily life to bring greater awareness of our internal world and closer connection to God, and ultimately a more Christlike mind. First, however, we look at some contemporary expressions of these traditions in the writings of modern Christian contemplatives.

6

Modern Christian Contemplatives

The twentieth century saw a reawakening of interest in Christian contemplative prayer and meditation. This occurred first in Catholicism and then spread to Protestantism. What is even more interesting is that at the start of the twenty-first century, we are seeing the spiritual disciplines and contemplative prayer strategies come into mainstream evangelicalism. This change is most probably a reaction against the emphasis on rational thought that is a core value of modernity, and because a postmodern worldview makes people more open to explore new ways of expressing faith. It addresses the weakness of focusing only on thinking and knowledge, as these things alone cannot produce the necessary transformation that is essential to being a follower of Christ.

This chapter looks at the contributions of three people: Thomas Merton, Richard Rohr and Dallas Willard.[1] Their work reshapes older mystic thinking and plants it firmly in a contemporary context.

Some readers might be concerned that the majority of this material has been drawn from Catholic tradition. However, it is not limited to this heritage. Dallas Willard has been the most influential Protestant evangelical writer, but he is not alone. An

---

1 Merton, *New Seeds of Contemplation*; Rohr, *The Naked Now*; Willard, *Hearing God*.

emphasis on spiritual disciplines has also been championed by Richard Foster and John Ortberg.[2] And the application of these practices has been encouraged by people such as James Bryan Smith.[3] These disciplines and practices have become popular because there has been a growing awareness of the lack of integration between our knowledge about God and our connection to God. In the same way, they teach us to be more aware and connected to our self. These are positive contributions to the way we live out our faith.

THOMAS MERTON: *NEW SEEDS OF CONTEMPLATION* AND *SPIRITUAL DIRECTION AND MEDITATION*

Thomas Merton revitalised interest in spiritual direction, meditation and contemplation in the twentieth century. He converted to Catholicism while studying at Columbia University in the United States and became a Cistercian monk, entering the Abbey of Gethsemani in 1941. During the twenty-seven years that he lived at the monastery, he became deeply involved in the American peace movement and was a strong supporter of the non-violent civil rights movement. During the later years of his life he became interested in Eastern religions and the dialogue between East and West. He died prematurely by accidental electrocution while travelling in Thailand at the age of fifty-three. He has left us a legacy of over sixty books, many poems and numerous articles on spirituality and social and political issues.

One of Merton's most influential books, *Spiritual Direction and Meditation*,[4] was in large part responsible for revitalising Christian

---

2 Foster, *Celebration of Discipline*; Ortberg, *The Life You've Always Wanted*.
3 Smith, *The Good and Beautiful God*.
4 Merton, *Spiritual Direction and Meditation*.

forms of meditation. He defines meditation as a reflective practice that involves a person's whole being: heart and mind, thought and love. Meditation is a means to intimately experience God and live this knowledge in our lives so that it is a reality and not just a fact. 'Meditative thought is simply the beginning of a process which leads to interior prayer and is normally supposed to culminate in contemplation and in affective communion with God.'[5]

Meditation is more than just thinking about things. It is a search for truth through knowledge and love. Each person will have a different way of practising prayer and meditation that is determined by their personality. The 'how' of this practice is less important than the end goal, which is to focus on the love of God as seen in the life of the incarnate Christ. When words come to an end, it is possible just to rest, which is a higher form of prayer.

In Merton's view, the subject of meditation can be focused on a mystery of the Christian faith or on ourselves, our problems and our experiences. Reflecting upon these practical aspects of life acknowledges God's presence and activity in our daily living. But it goes further, because we need to have a social and political awareness of our society to be able to meditate on contemporary events and how they relate to what is written in the Bible, and to place them in the context of the life, death and resurrection of Christ. A defining feature of Christian meditation for Merton is that inner transformation comes through inner awareness, brought about by the power of God's Spirit speaking to us in our consciousness.

In a second book, *New Seeds of Contemplation*, Merton explores the contemplative life that is available to every person. For him, 'con-

---

5 Ibid.

templation is, above all, awareness of the reality of the Source.'[6] Knowing God and finding our true self is intertwined.

He writes that solitude needs to be attained within our society and not in total isolation and withdrawal from the world. It is necessary so that we can love other people and understand the injustices and pain of the world. He also warns that being part of the masses, lost in the world and uncritically conforming to society, is a type of harmful solitude. Mindlessly living in this state deadens us to relationship with other people.

When we stop prizing our own actions and reputation, we become free to serve God for his sake alone. Selflessness enables us to find our true self, and this self is love, just as God is love. We cannot find God by shutting ourselves off from reality and retreating into our own mind: 'The man who locks himself up in private with his own selfishness has put himself into a position where the evil within him will either possess him like a devil or drive him out of his head.'[7]

Merton acknowledges that when we pray and meditate, our mind fills up with distractions from our imagination and memory. This is to be expected. The solution is to keep a simple attention towards God and keep our will orientated to God. All else that is going on in our mind can be allowed to occur in the background, like a movie. He says that one reason why people get frustrated in this type of prayer is because they try to control and stop this background noise, which only serves to make it worse.

To succeed in this contemplation is to find, in the nothingness of ourselves, the light of Christ. It requires the stripping down of our false selves, which is an utterly uncomfortable and dark place to go.

---

6 Ibid., p. 1.
7 Ibid., p. 79.

This is why many people prefer to run back to a form of spiritual business where they can see obvious results for their effort.

Reading Merton's work is enlightening because it grapples comprehensively with the theology behind Christian contemplative prayer practice. While Merton does go into the practicalities of how to practise meditative prayer, understanding the steps involved is a little like chasing after the wind. Just when you think that you have got the idea of how to do it, it becomes intangible again. This is partly intentional, because he wants us to avoid using a recipe that would blinker our practice and make it lifeless and desert-like.

When we compare his writing to mindful connection to the present, we find commonalities. Meditation is about intentional focus. It is natural for our minds to wander, and when they do we need to accept this and redirect our focus back to the topic of our meditation. Some days we will find this easier than others. The topic and method of our focus will be determined by what is happening in our life, where we are in our understanding of God, our reading of Scripture and what is happening in our society. Sometimes this focus will use our senses and imagination; at other times it will be more conceptual and intuitive.

Merton integrates meditation into our prayer time. This is like merging our mental, or rational, prayer with a form of meditation that is more like using the observing self. It allows space to be with God in silence and listen to God's Spirit. Through contemplation, our prayer, even if it starts by focusing on our own problems, will ultimately lead us back to God.

Merton critiques a type of mindful connection, or meditation, that is separate from God and disconnected from our world. He states that 'this business of doping your mind and isolating yourself from everything that lives, merely deadens you.[8] He also challenges the idea of using mindfulness and meditation to achieve a state of happiness and enlightenment. Our lives need to be God focused. A Christ-centred form of meditation and mindfulness should connect us three ways: to God, to our own thoughts and emotions, and to the world around us. The result will be transformation based on the life, death and resurrection of Christ, individually and within our society.

RICHARD ROHR: *THE NAKED NOW*

Richard Rohr was born in 1943, in Kansas, in the United States. He grew up in a conservative German Catholic family and was influenced by the Vatican Council II's reforms, the rise of psychology and social justice movements that focused on reforming US society in the 1960s.

Rohr is the founder of the Centre for Action and Contemplation. His writing is influenced by psychology, theology, philosophy, the mystic traditions of all religions, his practice of spiritual direction and his social experiences. He works against dualistic thinking and tries to encourage people to hold opposing thoughts in tension, with gracious acceptance. His intent is to recapture and revitalise forgotten aspects of Christian faith that can help us to go deeper in our experience of God.

In his book *The Naked Now*, Rohr poses a collection of insights to challenge us to learn a new way of seeing the world.[9] His work shows where Christianity forgot its mystic tradition, and he endeavours to recapture it and apply it to our current thinking.

---

8 Ibid., p. 64.
9 Rohr, *The Naked Now*.

Rohr suggests a need for us to go beyond our normal modes of thinking to think differently about the significant issues of life. He calls this way contemplation, a 'third eye of seeing', or prayer; 'It is a non-dualistic way of seeing the moment.'[10] He uses the word 'prayer' broadly to include practices that allow us to experience faith, hope and love. We can surrender ourselves to 'the naked now of true prayer' and bring ourselves before God.[11] God works in us through the Holy Spirit, and we become mirrors of God; we join in with the work that God has already begun. To do this there exists a paradox, that in losing our life in God we actually become more fully ourselves.

Rohr writes about the relationship between God's name and breathing. God calls himself 'I am' – 'Yahweh' in Exodus 3:14–15. Historically, the name Yahweh was considered an unspeakable name to the Jews. In everyday life they did not use this word for God but used an alternate name, Elohim or Adonai. Although the name Yahweh was not spoken, it could be breathed. The sound of this word is similar to breathing in and out, and breathing is central to life. This makes even more sense when we consider the act of breathing is linked to the creative act of the Spirit in Genesis (Gen 2:7) and to Jesus' breathing of the Spirit over the disciples (Jn 20:21–23). The use of breath can therefore be one aspect of prayer.

Rohr considers that there are three ways of seeing. The first is through the senses. The second uses imagination, intuition and reason. The third way goes further, doing these two things and then 'tasting' the experience and connecting to it.[12] This third way of seeing, where heart, mind and bodily awareness are all present, is what the mystics practised, and have also been called meditation and con-

10 Ibid., p. 12.
11 Ibid., p. 19.
12 Ibid., p. 27.

templation. This way of seeing moves us to inner experience. He refers to this process as transformation or holiness.

Rohr argues that Western culture's preference to ignore this third way of knowing is one of the main causes of black-and-white, or dualistic, thinking. All-or-nothing thinking can be fine for everyday life, but it is ineffective when we face suffering or complex issues. For these things, we need to move towards an acceptance of chaos and see things differently. Jesus modelled this by being content in the midst of life and retaining a sense of peace, despite the suffering around him. Rohr argues that this type of contemplation was taught in pre-Reformation Christianity, before the Enlightenment and before the Catholic Church became institutionalised. It has been neglected since. As a result, most people have not learned about wisdom, paradox and mystery, which are part of faith.

Rohr critiques the impact individualism has had on Western culture and how the style of Christianity presented by the church has failed to take a holistic approach. Focusing on the individual, it has failed to see larger community issues. Dualistic thinking has resulted in a divide between people, resulting in sexism, racism and other forms of division, to the point where wars have been fought based on doctrinal divisions. The emptiness of this approach has been a contributing factor to people walking away from their Christian tradition and looking for answers elsewhere, in other religions and psychology.

The alternative he proposes is to learn to sit in wonder, rather than be quick to answer. This requires a suspension of the judging, or rational, mind, which seeks to categorise, control and label our experiences. Learning to sit in wonder is to be open to new thoughts and experiences through acceptance, and it requires silence and peace. It is in this space that God meets us and transformation of the self can occur. Rohr refers to this concept of being still and turning off our rational mind as 'being present', and he illustrates it with the story of Mary and Martha, where Mary was present by sitting at Jesus' feet, listening and attending to him, not being busy and unreachable. This action of being fully present in the moment is related to wisdom.

Central to our ability to see the world in a non-dualistic way is the process of conversion, which Rohr views as intellectual, moral and religious. The end of this process should result in a person who can be present, seek the common good rather than be motivated by personal gain, and be a person of love. He highlights the fact that Jesus' call to repentance in Matthew 4:17 uses the word *metanoia*, which means 'change your mind.'[13] Conversion and repentance are about changing our mind and growing. He suggests that religion goes wrong where it merely provides us with new behaviours, beliefs and places to belong but does not create deep and lasting inner transformation.

This new way of being is related to Jesus' proclamation of the kingdom of God (Luke) or kingdom of Heaven (Matthew). In Rohr's view, this kingdom is not a place. It is a way of seeing and thinking – the naked now – that informs our action. With this orientation, the way we see the world is transformed socially and in every other aspect of life. In this context, prayer is not just a one-way conversation; it is more about tuning into God and developing an ability to listen. We are changed in the process and begin to join in with the work God has already started.

Using another metaphor, contemplative awareness is like the tree of life in the creation story, as opposed to the tree of knowledge that leads to dualistic thinking. In order to gain wisdom, we need to develop an ability to hold opposing views in tension and forgive the imperfection that exists in the world.

---

13 Ibid., p. 89.

This contemplative mindset does not divide, but handles truth humbly. It can hold ideas in tension and allows a person to practise forgiveness, humility, kindness, patience and compassion. This is ultimately what it means to have the mind of Christ. In Rohr's view, spiritual transformation is not about our morality or rational beliefs.

Perhaps the most difficult concept of Rohr's to understand is what he means by being awake, or conscious, which Rohr refers to as the True Self, the soul, our consciousness or our absolute attention. This True Self frees a person to be connected and caring, not driven by thoughts and feelings. This is a perceptual shift Rohr calls conversion. The thinking self no longer has such a hold, and we can stop analysing and categorising and just be. For Christians, this concept overlaps with the idea of the indwelling of the Holy Spirit. Both the Holy Spirit and our own spirit begin to see with a united eye.

To access this new thinking, we need to be able to hold the tension of this paradox. Mere logic cannot explain all things. It is possible for some things to be both true. For example, Jesus was both divine and human. The Trinity is both three and one. To persist in demanding either/or is to reject such paradoxes. Thinking in the naked now means accepting contradictory concepts and holding them in tension. It helps us avoid dualistic thinking. Being a Christian is less about belonging to a religion and adhering to a set of beliefs as being on a journey of transformation and living out our faith.

This transformation impacts the world around us and how we see things. It allows us to see the contradictions in ourselves and other people, accepting that we are not all good. This frees us to love ourselves and other people unconditionally.

Rohr's *Naked Now* helpfully provides an intellectual scaffolding to understand the way our Christian mystic tradition was neglected and forgotten in the West. With the institutionalisation of the church and the rise of rational thinking, we have belittled our conscious mind, valuing factual truth above all things. The result is that we can become trapped in a modern dualist mindset and black-and-white thinking. In the right context there is nothing wrong with using this rational part of our mind, but when it dominates over all else it leads to inflexibility and the neglect of connection with the present.

Aspects of Rohr's teaching should be approached with caution. While his explanations are helpful in bridging the gap between historical Christian contemplative prayer practice and mindful connection, at times his argument can blur the line between Eastern mysticism and Christian mysticism. There are similarities between the two, but in an effort to cease dualistic thinking, this approach might be a little too assimilative and can lead us down the path of wondering why being Christian is so important.

It is also hard to reconcile Rohr's interchangeable use of conversion, the Holy Spirit indwelling us and the concept of being fully present. In my view, conversion is about making a decision to follow Christ. The Spirit then dwells in us, and we need to learn to listen in the present to the connection between God's Spirit and our own. Further to this, not all followers of Christ are naturally good at connecting with the present. Living in the naked now is more a process to be learned over time as we mature. Only when we conceptualise conversion as a continuous process rather than a once-in-a-lifetime decision can these ideas go together. It is, however, helpful to realise that the Spirit joins with us in this practice, meeting with and speaking to our deep consciousness.

Rohr's concept of the naked now is generally helpful because it can allow us make sense of the overlap between mindful connection to the present and contemplative prayer, and how this practice influences faith, self-knowledge and our relationship with God. Rohr also brings us back continually to the example and attitude of Jesus and his teachings. He adds to this with insights into Christian mystical thought and practice. One particularly helpful aspect relates to the focus on the breath, and the significance of this in Scripture and for our understanding of God. Rohr's work challenges us to look with fresh eyes at Jesus' way of seeing and relating to the world. He does not use black-and-white thinking, and to the annoyance of those around him often resists compartmentalising judgements and ideas.

Rohr teaches us that as we journey through our own faith, we are changed and develop the ability to accept reality and hold ideas in tension. We gradually become more closely connected with the present and with God's Spirit as it works in the world. We become the new kingdom here on earth.

DALLAS WILLARD: *HEARING GOD*

Dallas Willard was born in the United States in 1935. He was a Southern Baptist minister and wrote many books that focused on spiritual discipline and faith experience. He was also an influential author and teacher, and professor of Philosophy at the University of Southern California.

Willard's 2012 book, *Hearing God*, is based on the same understanding of faith and Christian life as that adopted by Brother Lawrence. Willard's aim is to provide ordinary Christians with a language and framework for living out an ongoing, two-way relationship with God that includes both listening and speaking.

Willard centres the discussion of relationship with God around the concept of abiding, as found in the Gospel of John. The evidence that this relationship is at the centre of our life is shown in personal transformation as we become more like Christ.

Prayer in the context of this relationship is an honest exchange between God and our self. To have a loving relationship we need to love God with our heart, mind, soul and strength. In doing this we will begin to understand what God actually wants and we will act upon his will. We see evidence of people who had this type of relationship with God in the Bible, and we must assume that what happened in the lives of these people can also occur in ours. This presupposes that we actually read and study the Bible regularly. We also need to pray for the faith to believe that God can speak to us in the same way he did to these people in the past.

Living in the continual presence of God means that we are never alone. In our modern culture, being lonely is one of the things we most fear. Alienation from God and the world leaves us in a dark place. The kind of relationship Willard says we can have with God means that loneliness is never possible, as nothing can separate us from God's love or presence with us.

Discerning God's presence is something gained through experience and practice. Sometimes it can be sensed; at other times it is obvious because God acts in conjunction with our actions. God also speaks to us individually through our relationship with him as well as to groups of people. This happens because we are in relationship with God and have a shared understanding, like friends or collaborators. We know each other's wants and needs and work to make things happen accordingly.

Life lived in God's presence defines the purpose of our existence. 'This union with God consists chiefly in a conversational relationship with God while we are consistently and deeply engaged as his friend and collaborater in the affairs of the kingdom of the heavens.[14] Other forms of feeling God's presence are important, but they are never as essential as God's communicating to us through word and shared activity. This is because when we understand God's purpose, we willingly identify with Christ.

Some people doubt that God speaks to them, but in Willard's view this might be more to do with the failure to separate God's speaking from whether we are actually tuned in to what he is saying so that we can hear it. It is necessary for us to be willing and ready to put into action what God says. If we are not, then there is little point in God speaking to us. If we have not made the decision to give up our life in total surrender to God, then God's speaking to us is futile because our real intention is to live for ourselves regardless of anything else. Even if none of these issues concern us, many people still struggle with our Western worldview that is based on the observed, scientific realm and does not allow space for God to act in the world or speak to us. The result is a view of God that is disconnected and not relational.

The usual way God communicates to people is through a still small voice (1 Kgs 19:11–13), which has been referred to as the inner voice, or the interior voice, or our Spirit. This voice might not always be recognised as anything significant. People who regularly hear it usually do not speak about it publicly. 'The Scripture teaches that the less dramatic the message, the fuller the content and the more advanced the person who is receiving the message.'[15] God does not try to grab our attention loudly. If we are not listening, we are likely to miss what God is saying. God's Spirit speaks most commonly in and through the words of other people to us, and within our own spirit, in our thoughts and feelings.

---

14 Willard, *Hearing God*, p. 75.
15 Ibid., p. 118.

So God uses our self-knowledge or self-awareness, which is heightened and given a special quality by his presence and direction, to search us out and reveal to us the truth about ourselves and our world. And we are able to use his knowledge of himself – made available to us in Christ and the Scriptures – to understand in some measure his thoughts and intentions toward us and to help us see his workings in our world.[16]

As we grow in our faith, God's law and ways become part of our being so that we become more like God in every way. Our spirit's awareness brings our thoughts and actions into line with God's. This awareness of our spirit extends to every part of our life: our family, work, thoughts, feelings and behaviour.

So the thoughts and feelings in the mind and spirit of one who is surrendered to God should be treated as if God were walking through one's personality with a candle, directing one's attention to things one after the other. As we become used to the idea that God is friendly and helpful, that he desires to straighten, inform and correct for our good as well as to comfort and encourage and that he really does love us, then we can begin to pray heartily with the psalmist, 'Search me, O God, and know my heart; test me and know my thoughts' (Ps 139: 23).[17]

This conversational relationship extends to the way we pray. We do not just say prayers of petition but are open to God's guidance in what we are to pray, which is a form of listening. When it comes to loving other people, God directs us to know what their needs are so that we can express love fully to them.

When we want God to speak to us in more spectacular ways by visions, dreams or an audible voice, this often reflects an immaturity of character and faith. These things do happen, but to value them over and above the regular silent guidance of God in our life is flawed.

---

16 Ibid., p. 131.
17 Ibid., p. 135.

We cannot learn to hear and understand God's individual word to us without first understanding Scripture and immersing our mind in it. 'It is through the action of the word of God upon us, throughout us and with us that we come to have the mind of Christ and thus to live fully in the kingdom of God.'[18] We can become more familiar with God's mind through reading Scripture – with an attitude of prayer so that the contents deeply work in our life and become real. 'We read to open ourselves to the Spirit.'[19] As the contents of Scripture are transferred and imparted into our deep self, Christ's mind becomes our mind.

We need our minds to be transformed so that all the false ideas, thoughts and habits are washed out of them. Christ changes these patterns through his word in us, developing in us the character necessary to hear what God wants to say to us.

> Christ through his word removes the old routines in the heart and mind – the old routines of thought, feeling, action, imagination, conceptualization, belief, inference – and in their place he puts something else: his thoughts, his attitudes, his beliefs, his ways of seeing and interpreting things, his words. He washes out our minds, and in the place of confusion and falsehood – or hatred, suspicion and fear, to speak of emotions – he brings clarity, truth, love, confidence and hopefulness.[20]

The communication between our self and God grows in intimacy over time, so that it becomes a communing relationship and ultimately a union. This brings us back to the idea of the vine and branches, where our being grafted into the vine allows us to abide with Christ, to know his thoughts and life in us. It is also reflected in

18 Ibid., p. 192.
19 Ibid., p. 212.
20 Ibid., pp. 199–200.

Paul's statement that we have the mind of Christ (1 Cor 2:16). This new life in Christ makes us fully alive. We become transformed, new people. This new way of being is a choice and requires our will to remain in it.

Willard's *Hearing God* is grounded in a modern worldview and is rational and reasoned. It emphasises the centrality of the Word of God, where meditation on Scripture together with a relationship with God is the foundation for being able to hear God's voice in our everyday lives. His argument is inspired by the work of Brother Lawrence and borrows heavily from Jesus' teaching in the gospel of John.

Much of Willard's argument is balanced by the meditation exercises interspersed throughout the theory. These *lectio divina* exercises are based on the tradition of St Ignatius and follow five steps: information, longing, affirmation, invocation and appropriation. The passage of Scripture is read and reread, allowing it to penetrate deeply into our life to initiate change. In bringing this discipline into the mainstream of evangelical Christian faith, Willard makes what would normally be considered a Catholic practice accessible to a greater number of people. While it is not the same as other aspects of contemplative prayer, it brings an important balance between emphasis on the word of God and prayer.

Willard tries to resolve the issue of how God's voice fits into our physical, science-based reality. He uses examples from physics to support his argument, trying to find a way to support the possibility that God can speak directly to the human mind:

> In trying to understand the great power of words we cannot afford to overlook their spiritual nature. Spirit is unbodied, personal force. It is personal reality that can and often does work independently of physical or bodily forces. It can also work in conjunction with them. We

can most clearly see spirit in our own selves as the force that belongs to thought, emotion and intention. In the biblical view, spirit reaches far beyond these – and beyond our limited understanding – and ultimately serves as the foundation of all reality. 'God is spirit' (Jn 4:24).[21]

Willard's teachings in the area are somewhat confusing. What might be more consistent, biblically and physically, is an understanding that humans have a spirit that gives them life within, but with which God's Spirit can commune. Our understanding of neuroscience and the 'self' identifies this as our consciousness. In this context, Willard's idea that words are spiritual powers makes more sense. It is not that they are independent powers, but that they have power and can be guided on a spiritual level. Similarly, the voice of God communicates to us on this same level of our consciousness.

One of Willard's most interesting contributions is the way he provides context, not just for hearing God's voice but also the opposite reality: hearing the voice of evil. While controversial, this logical acknowledgement that our minds can be influenced by God and evil using the same mechanism meshes with the spiritual reality that is accepted in many non-Western cultures. It brings a secondary basis for the possibility that meditation can bring us closer to God and bring Christlike transformation, but can also open us up to a realm of spiritual forces that the West has long decided are irrelevant superstition and which do not exist. On a purely logical level, if meditation can open our consciousness up to influence from more than one source, it is important that we decide whether we want this to be God or a different, opposing spiritual presence.

---

21 Ibid., p. 157.

THE CONTEMPORARY CONTRIBUTION

The progressive thinking of Merton, Rohr and Willard breaks meditation and contemplative prayer out of its traditional isolated practice and brings it into the everyday, broadening it from mere individualistic transformation to concerns for social justice and participation in God's work in the world. We are challenged not to rely only on our knowledge of God, but to go deeper, letting the Spirit work in the innermost parts of our self to create transformation.

While I generally find these teachings encouraging and stretching, I struggle with some of the more Catholic understandings of God and find some of Rohr's ideas a little too liberal in approach. But this does not have to take away from their overall helpfulness. Discernment is required. I do believe that Willard raises an important point that indiscriminate use of mindfulness and meditation can actually open us up to evil if we are unwise about our practice. This is why it is so important that mindfulness is not used without a clear base in values and worldview. For Christians, it needs to be practiced in the context of a relationship with Christ, where our spirit (the observing self) abides and can hear the Spirit of God.

In Part III of this book, we explore how to apply these modern Christian contemplative practices to Christ-centred mindfulness.

Practising Christ-Centred Mindfulness

7

The Basics of Mindful Connection to the Present

But Jesus called for them and said, 'Let the little children come to me, and do not stop them; for it is to such as these that the kingdom of God belongs. Truly I tell you, whoever does not receive the kingdom of God as a little child will never enter it.'

Luke 18:16–17

When I was a young child, I was given a book called *Discovering Our World*.[1] It was all about the amazing things God had created and was unusual in that it explored and captured the world from the viewpoint of a curious child using all their senses. It looked at the colours of flowers and leaves, the pattern of lines on our fingerprint, and the unique textures, shapes and colours of insects. When you watch little children exploring nature, this is what they do. They engage fully with the sensory experience. They are curious, open and interested, and have a sense of wonder at what they see. This child-like attitude captures an important part of what mindful connection is, and the mindset you need to bring to its practice.

---

1 Doney, *Discovering Our World*.

Mindful connection uses the observing self. This part of our mind has been called other names, but essentially it is the silent part of our mind that observes what is happening both within us and around us. It is related to the concept of consciousness. Regardless of what changes are occurring in our body or environment, this observing self stays the same.

Think of the sky. From day to night, the colours and appearance of the sky change. Similarly, the weather patterns within it are constantly changing. But the sky stays the same and does not change. So it is with the observing self. This metaphor can help us to understand the concept more deeply.

We are more familiar with the other part of our mind known as the rational self. This part makes judgements about things, remembers, categorises and worries (Table 7.1). It tends to dominate our thinking, with the unhelpful side effect that we often get hooked by our thoughts and believe them even when they are unhealthy or not correct. This rational part of our mind is like the weather patterns and the transitions between night and day that transform the appearance of the sky. They are forever changing.

This understanding of the rational and observing self is based on ACT. The observing self is the means by which we fully engage with the present moment, mindfully connecting with what is happening in the now. Developing our observing self brings healthy balance to our thinking so that we are more aware of our inner experiences. When we are more aware, we are able to make choices that are value driven and not dictated by a thought, emotion or physical sensation. Transformation of our thoughts, emotions and behaviours becomes possible when we use the observing self to increase our awareness of

Rational self	Observing self
Internal dialogue	Consciousness
Thoughts	Connection through our senses
Judgements	Absolute attention
Comparisons	Naked now
Knowledge	Wisdom
Memories	Space where God's Spirit speaks to us

Table 7.1. Forms and names used to describe the rational and observing self

what we are experiencing, and then use the techniques of expansion and defusion to enable us to live by our values.

The observing self has been called other names in contemplative prayer practice. These include the naked now, the third eye of seeing, our consciousness, wisdom, the true self and absolute attention (Table 7.1).[2]

The Christian mystic tradition and Scripture can further expand this understanding by adding a theological viewpoint. The observing self is the space where our spirit communes with the Spirit of God. And, transformation is not just based on our choices and actions – it is made possible through the power of the Holy Spirit.

The practice of Christ-centred mindfulness requires the discipline to use the observing self to connect to the present using our five senses or imagination and to focus on one thing (Figure 7.1). We need to accept that we will become distracted from this task by thoughts, memories and interruptions, but when this happens we need to notice what is happening and then gently redirect our focus back to one thing.

2 Rohr, *The Naked Now*.

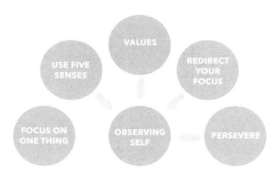

Figure 7.1. Skills required when using the observing self to mindfully connect to the present

This final section of the book takes the idea of mindful connection, as used in ACT and Christian mysticism, and uses it to create practical exercises that are Christ-centred. I have grouped these exercises into three broad collections. The first introduces the concepts of connection to the present, defusion, acceptance and expansion as found in ACT. I have rewritten these so that they are more integrated with faith. The second collection provides a variety of exercises based on our five senses. The third collection reinvents and interprets the Christian mystic tradition and makes it accessible in a contemporary format.

These practices can be used by followers of Christ to bring greater connection with the present moment, to develop a deeper understanding of thoughts, feelings and behaviours, and to move towards greater psychological health. These exercises can also be used to develop the discipline of silently listening to God. The ultimate aim is to deepen our love for God and, in doing so, transform our self and the world around us.

8

ACTing to Create Change

Be still and know that I am God.
Psalm 46:10

MINDFUL CONNECTION WITH THE PRESENT MOMENT

Plugging back into the present moment and connecting with our surroundings does not need to be complicated. It tends to prove most difficult when we are troubled with a major life problem, loss or trauma. Problems have the habit of filling our minds and taking over our thoughts to the point where we can be emotionally and mentally absent from the people around us. This impacts our relationships in destructive ways. Similarly, loss can leave us cycling through numbness, shock, anger and sadness, to the point where we feel completely adrift and removed from the events that are happening around us. For those of us who have experienced trauma, the emotions that come back with remembering things associated with the original pain can be either intensely overwhelming or leave us numb, disconnected and absent.

Trying any of these three exercises will help you reverse these reactions and get you back to present reality.

USE YOUR SENSES

Stop.

Be still.

Force yourself to name out loud, or quietly in your head:

Five things you can see.

Five things you can hear.

Five things you can feel or touch.

PHYSICALLY GROUND YOURSELF

Stop.

Be still.

Push your feet into the ground.

Straighten your back.

Put your shoulders back and your head up.

Use your five senses to connect to your environment.

STOP AND RELAX

Stop.

Be still.

Take five deep breaths.

Slow your breathing down.

Breathe from your belly.

Breathe deeply.

Continue until you are calm.

MINDFUL ENCOUNTERS WITH GOD'S CREATION

When I look at your heavens, the work of your fingers,
the moon and the stars that you have established;
what are human beings that you are mindful of them,
mortals that you care for them?
Psalm 8:3–4

Mindful connection in its simplest form is about engaging with what is happening around you with all your senses. It does not need to be fancy. It just needs to get you tuned in with the 'now'. There are some basic ways you can practise this connection throughout your day so that you are not distracted by thoughts and feelings. The more you practice, the easier you will find this skill, and the more you will be aware when you have disengaged and gone to another place in your mind.

The following mindful activities specifically encourage a curiosity and awareness of nature. For people who follow Christ, these exercises can foster in us a wonder at God's creation and the nature of the Creator. The end of this process should lead us to praise.

PETS

Sit quietly with your pet, whether they be a cat or dog, or perhaps something more unusual like a snake, guinea pig, rat or chicken.

Hold them and stroke their feathers, fur or scales. What do they feel like? What is their temperature like? Is their skin rough, or fur smooth? Does the feel change over the surface of their body as you stroke them?

What do they look like? Observe their colour and texture. What colour are their eyes? Do they look happy?

As you interact with them, are they making some sort of noise? What is it? Listen carefully.

Notice whether they have their own unique smell. What do they smell like?

As you do this exercise, you will notice that your mind will wander and start thinking about other things. When you notice this is happening, gently redirect your focus back to your pet and continue to be present by observing them and fully engaging in your relationship with them.

WALKING IN THE PARK

Go for a walk in your favourite local park. As you are walking, try to engage your observing self by looking at what is happening around you. Do not block your thoughts or try to push them away, but instead notice their presence and gently direct your attention to your surroundings.

What is the weather like today? Is the sky grey or blue, cloudy or clear? What is the temperature like? Can you feel the wind flowing around your body?

Try taking a breath. As you slowly breathe in, what can you smell? Can you smell the trees or flowers, or maybe freshly cut grass?

If you open your mouth, can you taste the air? What does it taste like?

Can you hear the birds in the trees? Are there any people or pets around? What other noises can you hear?

Look carefully at the plants and trees in the park. What is the texture like in the bark? What colour are the leaves?

While you are doing this exercise, try to just notice your surroundings. Each time your thoughts distract you, gently refocus your attention on observing the natural world around you.

SITTING AT THE BEACH

You can do this task either walking or sitting quietly on the sand.

Start by looking at your surroundings. What can you see? How many colours can you see in the water – blue, green, grey? What is being reflected in the water? Is the sea smooth and peaceful or rough and menacing?

Can you feel anything on your skin? The warmth of the sun? A cold or hot wind? The spray from the sea?

Can you smell the ocean? What other things can you smell? Perhaps there is seaweed?

What sounds are around you? Are there smashing waves, the squawks of seagulls?

Take a closer look. What can you see in the sand and the rocks around you? Take time to explore the shells and small creatures nearby. Pick things up and feel their texture, shape and weight. If you have bare feet, what can you feel?

Engage with this experience like a child who is exploring something for the first time. When your thoughts, memories or feelings distract you, gently refocus on observing the environment around you.

When you complete these tasks, read Psalm 104 (or one of your choice) and spend some time praising God for his creation.

Bless the LORD, O my soul.
O LORD my God, you are very great.
You are clothed with honour and majesty,
wrapped in light as with a garment.
You stretch out the heavens like a tent,
you set the beams of your chambers on the waters,
you make the clouds your chariot,
you ride on the wings of the wind,
you make the winds your messengers,
fire and flame your ministers.
You set the earth on its foundations,
so that it shall never be shaken.
...
May the glory of the LORD endure for ever;

may the LORD rejoice in his works –
who looks on the earth and it trembles,
who touches the mountains and they smoke.
I will sing to the LORD as long as I live;
will sing praise to my God while I have being.
May my meditation be pleasing to him,
for I rejoice in the LORD.
Let sinners be consumed from the earth,
and let the wicked be no more.
Bless the LORD, O my soul.
Praise the LORD![1]

MINDFUL CONNECTION TO EVERYDAY TASKS

Now before the festival of the Passover, Jesus knew that his hour had come to depart from this world and go to the Father. Having loved his own who were in the world, he loved them to the end. The devil had already put it into the heart of Judas son of Simon Iscariot to betray him. And during supper Jesus, knowing that the Father had given all things into his hands, and that he had come from God and was going to God, got up from the table, took off his outer robe, and tied a towel around himself. Then he poured water into a basin and began to wash the disciples' feet and to wipe them with the towel that was tied around him. He came to Simon Peter, who said to him, 'Lord, are you going to wash my feet?' Jesus answered, 'You do not know now what I am doing, but later you will understand.' Peter said to him, 'You will never wash my feet.' Jesus answered, 'Unless I wash you, you have no share with me.' Simon Peter said to him, 'Lord, not my feet only but also my hands and my head!' Jesus said to him, 'One who has bathed does not need to wash, except for the feet, but is entirely clean. And you are clean, though not all of you.' For he knew who was to betray him; for this reason he said, 'Not all of you are clean.'

---

1 Psalm 104:1–5, 31–35.

After he had washed their feet, had put on his robe, and had returned to the table, he said to them, 'Do you know what I have done to you? You call me Teacher and Lord – and you are right, for that is what I am. So if I, your Lord and Teacher, have washed your feet, you also ought to wash one another's feet. For I have set you an example, that you also should do as I have done to you. Very truly, I tell you, servants are not greater than their master, nor are messengers greater than the one who sent them. If you know these things, you are blessed if you do them.

John 13:1–17

Most of us, if we are really honest, dislike the ordinary grind of household jobs. After all, there is a reason why we call them chores or housework. There are the jobs we do to care for ourselves, like having a shower, brushing our teeth, doing our hair, working out what we will wear for the day, packing our bag. Then there are the jobs we do to care for those around us. These include feeding the pets, making the kids' lunches, putting a load of washing in the machine and hanging it on the line, making the bed. And we often do many of these things before we even leave the house in the morning. These are the necessities of life.

We often do these tasks absently. For example, how many times have you woken up and got into the shower and then out again, assuming you actually washed yourself but with no memory of having done so? You were operating on autopilot. Your mind had you off task, thinking about other things. And then there are all those times we have things to do but come to the task kicking and screaming because we do not want to do it. Instead of peacefully completing the task with a servant heart of acceptance and love, we waste an opportunity by spending the whole time we are doing it caught up in feelings of anger and resentment and thinking negative thoughts.

What do you think would happen if you changed the way you did these things? If you paid attention and connected with the experience and did these activities out of love? For jobs that are unpleasant, you might find that a mindful approach changes the way you experience them.

Choose a job you do around the house that is routine and ordinary and try to do it mindfully. You might like to adopt an attitude similar to an inquisitive child, observing details that you would not normally notice.

TAKING A SHOWER

Mindfully connect to what you are doing instead of blindly going through the motions.

Notice the sensation of dragging your clothing across your skin as you undress yourself. Notice any stiffness or pain in your body as you move, and the temperature on your skin from the air around you. Notice the sounds you can hear.

As you enter the shower, notice the feel of the steam on your face, the changing temperature of the water as you adjust the taps. Feel the sensation of the water splashing over your skin as you stand there.

Then as you wash yourself, soak up the feeling of the soap on your skin, and the feeling of the shampoo in your hair that travels down your face as you wash it out.

As you do this exercise, you will find your mind will drag you away to think about all the things you need to do when you are finished, and maybe problems with your family or work.

When this happens, notice the thoughts, and then gently re-direct your focus back to the shower. Use your five senses and observing self to simply focus and connect to what is happening in the present.

Try mindfully doing another task that you ordinarily struggle to complete because of a bad attitude. After you have completed it, take a moment to reflect on what you discovered. And then spend a moment contemplating Jesus' servant-hearted example. In what way does your experience plus Jesus' example challenge you to change how you do things, or perhaps the attitude you adopt while you are doing it?

The challenge is to practise a mindful attitude to life that is accepting, which allows us to fully experience the present moment. The more we do this, the less our minds will take us to another place. Over time our attitude to these mundane tasks will be transformed. If we adopt a similar attitude to Jesus, we will adopt a servant heart and be motivated by love.

MINDFUL CONNECTION TO BREATH

The God who made the world and everything in it, he who is Lord of heaven and earth, does not live in shrines made by human hands, nor is he served by human hands, as though he needed anything, since he himself gives to all mortals life and breath and all things. From one ancestor he made all nations to inhabit the whole earth, and he allotted the times of their existence and the boundaries of the places where they would live, so that they would search for God and perhaps grope for him and find him – though indeed he is not far from each one of us. For 'In him we live and move and have our being.'
Acts 17:24–28

Mindfulness of breath engages all the senses in observing the breath. This exercise integrates mindful connection to breath with our understanding of the Holy Spirit as Giver of Life and Spirit of Truth. In this way it is an active rather than a passive task. It is designed to bring your awareness to the present moment so you fully connect with your experience.

There are two variations of mindful breathing, and you are encouraged to try both and use the one that is best for you.

MINDFUL CONNECTION TO BREATH - SHORT FORM

Start this exercise by sitting in a comfortable position with your eyes closed.

Gently bring your focus to your breathing. Do not try to change your breathing, just notice the natural rise and fall of your chest as you breathe in and out. Take a few slow, deep breaths. Then try to slowly push all the air out of your lungs until they are completely empty. Your body will kick in with a reflex, naturally refilling your lungs. Let this happen without trying to control the refilling process.

Repeat these steps again, up to ten times. Each time, slowly breath out then let your lungs refill themselves.

As you breathe you will notice your mind distracting you. When this happens, gently redirect your focus back to your breathing. To finish this exercise, slowly open your eyes and reorientate yourself to your surroundings.

MINDFUL CONNECTION TO BREATH – EXTENDED VERSION

Start this exercise by sitting in a comfortable position with your eyes closed.

Gently bring your attention and focus to your breathing. Do not try to change your breathing, just notice the natural rise and fall of your chest.

Starting with your nose, notice the feel of the air coming into your nostrils. What temperature is that air? Can you feel the air across the skin on your face as you breathe? Does the air make a noise as you do this? Then move further inside and notice the air as it travels to the back of your nose and throat. What does it feel like? Continue further and move your focus to your chest. Are you breathing shallowly or deeply? Which part of your chest is moving? Feel the way your rib cage rises and falls with every breath.

Now continue to focus on your breath as you breathe in and out. During this exercise you will notice your rational mind trying to distract you by hooking you with thoughts, memories and worries. When this happens, notice each thought as it comes, then gently redirect your attention back to your breathing. Stay focused on your breath. Continue to breathe deeply for between five and ten minutes.

It is normal for your rational mind to keep interrupting this exercise. When this occurs, simply notice it happening and persist in gently redirecting your attention to the rise and fall of your breath.

As you bring this exercise to a close, reflect for a moment on the following verse:

> The spirit of God has made me,
> and the breath of the Almighty gives me life.
> Job 33:4

If you feel prompted, say a short prayer in response. When you are ready, reorientate your focus to your surroundings and open your eyes.

MINDFUL CONNECTION TO YOUR THOUGHTS

O LORD, you have searched me and known me.
You know when I sit down and when I rise up;
you discern my thoughts from far away.
You search out my path and my lying down,
and are acquainted with all my ways.
Even before a word is on my tongue,
O LORD, you know it completely.
You hem me in, behind and before,
and lay your hand upon me.
Such knowledge is too wonderful for me;
it is so high that I cannot attain it.

...

Search me, O God, and know my heart;
test me and know my thoughts.
See if there is any wicked way in me,
and lead me in the way everlasting.
Psalm 139:1–6, 23–24.

The observing self can be trained to create greater awareness of thoughts. This is the first step towards being able to interact with your thoughts in a healthy way.

MINDFUL CONNECTION TO YOUR THOUGHTS – SHORT FORM

Find a quiet place to sit down with your eyes shut. As you relax, scan your body to make sure you are in a comfortable position. You might need to move a little or adjust your posture.

When you are still and comfortable, imagine you are sitting or lying on a grassy hill looking up at a clear blue sky. You might like to imagine Christ is there with you, silent beside you and accepting, like a friend. As you look at the sky, every now and then clouds pass by.

In this exercise, focus on the sky and let the clouds pass. You will notice that, from time to time, thoughts will come into your head. It might be about what you are going to eat for dinner, or something you are doing tomorrow, or a worry or memory. When this happens, place these thoughts onto one of the passing clouds. Do not try to control these thoughts. Each time a thought occurs, simply place it on a cloud and let it pass through the sky.

Always redirect your attention to observing the sky. In this way you are not controlling or interacting with your thoughts, you are simply noticing them and letting them pass.

Continue this task for several minutes.

This mindful awareness of thoughts task can be undertaken using a variety of different metaphors. People tend to vary in their ability to use visual imagery. If you are someone who finds it difficult to think in pictures, you can close your eyes and imagine a blackboard. On this background your thoughts can appear in white chalk and then fade away like they are being rubbed off with a duster. Like all new skills, practice makes a lot of difference, and with perseverance this task becomes easier to master.

Other metaphors that you could use include:

- leaves flowing down a stream
- waves rolling onto a beach
- carriages on a freight train at a railway crossing
- birds flying past in the air
- water going down a waterfall
- a blank room with two doors – thoughts come in the left and out the right door.

Use the metaphor that you can visualise and relate to most easily.

Defusion

Another way to achieve mindful connection to your thoughts is through defusion, an ACT skill that enables you to create distance from a thought so that it will not hook you in and have you believing it wholeheartedly. Defusion helps you to have a greater degree of choice in how you respond to your thoughts. For followers of Christ, this means that you can stop and reflect on your faith and consider a response to these thoughts that is consistent with what you believe in.

Defusion techniques manipulate the thought – for example, by giving it a name. This creates distance between you and the thought. Then, as you manipulate the thought further, the power of the thought becomes less and less, until you repeat it to the point where it slowly becomes meaningless noise.

It is like holding a book right up to your face. While it is there, your field of vision is blocked and all you can see is an out-of-focus book, perhaps with a little peripheral vision around the outside. Everything directly in front of you is unseen. Then as you move this book further and further away from your face, more of your surroundings become visible. Eventually, by holding the book at arm's length, you can see all that is around you, including the book. This is the same as the process of defusion. When you are fused with a thought, all you know and believe is that thought. As you defuse from it, you gain the ability to hold that thought together with everything else that is around you, and its power is diminished.

MINDFUL CONNECTION TO YOUR THOUGHTS – EXTENDED VERSION

Be still

Find a quiet place to sit down with your eyes shut. As you relax, scan your body to make sure you are in a comfortable position. You might need to move a little or adjust your posture. Direct your attention to the sounds around you, and then gently redirect your attention to your breathing.

Picture your thought

Think of a recent time when a distressing or painful thought was on your mind. Take the time to remember the place where you were, what was happening and what this thought was. The thought might be a phrase, a word, a name you called yourself or a memory of something someone else said to you. It might be a painful problem that you are experiencing in your life.

Name your story

When you have a clear impression of this thought, give it a name. For example, if you thought 'I'm such a failure', you could name this the 'failure story'. Quietly acknowledge the presence of the 'failure story'.

Create distance

Next, imagine that this phrase or thought is playing on your television, iPad or smartphone. Visualise these words on the screen and imagine them being audible so you can hear them. As this is a special screen, you can manipulate the words of the phrase and their audible sound. First try changing the colour and font of the words. Make them bigger and then smaller again. Have a go at changing the way they sound. Slow the sound down, then speed it up. Change the volume. Try manipulating the sound and picture of your thought in other ways. For example, try to play the words of your thought in time with 'Twinkle, Twinkle, Little Star'. You can even try repeating it over and over until it sounds like meaningless noise.

Evaluate your thought

By this stage you might notice that the thought, which began as distressing, now has less power over you because you have defused from it. Focus once again on your thought. In

Psalm 139, David writes:

> *Search me, O God, and know my heart;*
> *test me and know my thoughts.*
> *See if there is any wicked way in me,*
> *and lead me in the way everlasting.*

Psalm 139: 23–24.

Place this thought alongside what you know of God and how he sees you, and ask God's Spirit to guide you in a response. Is your thought consistent with the values, promises and statements in the Bible? What do you think God would say to you in response?

Respond

Make a choice to do something that is consistent with your faith and values in response to your reflection. If it is meaningful to you, say a short prayer. When you have done this task, slowly bring you attention back to the sounds around you, then open your eyes. If you decided to follow through with an action or activity, do this now.

MINDFUL CONNECTION TO YOUR FEELINGS

One day [Jesus] got into a boat with his disciples, and he said to them, 'Let us go across to the other side of the lake.' So they put out, and while they were sailing he fell asleep. A gale swept down on the lake, and the boat was filling with water, and they were in danger. They went to him and woke him up, shouting, 'Master, Master, we are perishing!' And he woke up and rebuked the wind and the raging waves; they ceased, and there was a calm. He said to them, 'Where is

your faith?' They were afraid and amazed, and said to one another, 'Who then is this, that he commands even the winds and the water, and they obey him?'
Luke 8:22–25

Emotions and physical urges come and go like waves. For people who suffer worry, fear, anxiety or chronic physical illness and pain, these feelings can be overwhelming. The same can also be true when we feel emotions like loss, sadness and anger. Just as waves have a peak and trough, so these emotions build up and then dissipate over time. It is impossible for our body to continually keep us at the peak. Knowing that the highest point of any emotion will eventually pass can help us ride them like waves as a surfer does, rather than fearing that they will drown us.

Expansion

Expansion is an ACT skill that teaches us to allow painful emotions and ride them like a surfer rather than pushing them away. We can do this by making space for them within our internal experience.

MINDFUL CONNECTION TO YOUR FEELINGS – SHORT FORM

Try following these three steps when you experience a difficult feeling or uncomfortable physical sensation:

Stop. Be curious and notice what is happening. Use your five senses to observe what is going on within you.

Remember that emotions and physical urges are like waves. This will pass. You can ride this uncomfortable feeling until it becomes more bearable.

Breathe slowly and deeply. Try to breathe into the space where you feel the discomfort. Relax the space around it. Imagine that, as you breathe, you are making room for this emotion. Allow it to be there. Continue breathing deeply until the feeling subsides.

MINDFUL CONNECTION TO YOUR FEELINGS – EXTENDED VERSION[2]

Observe

Find somewhere to sit quietly and shut your eyes.

Imagine you are alone, sitting in a boat in the ocean. As the waves pass under your boat, you rise and fall gently. These waves are the changing emotions and physical urges in your body. Like the ocean, they change with the weather and affect the sailing of your boat.

Think back to an event or moment that was emotionally painful or physically uncomfortable. Try to bring the full experience to mind as it happened. If you are attending to a present physical sensation, fully focus on this. Be curious. Engage all your senses. Where in your body are you feeling this emotion or sensation? Does it have a temperature? Is it hot or cold, or maybe prickly? Does it have a colour? Are there any thoughts that accompany it?

---

2 Harris, *The Happiness Trap*, p. 14.

Now try to rate this sensation out of ten, where ten is really uncomfortable and one is fine. Feeling this unpleasant experience is like sitting in a boat in the midst of a storm where the waves are a deep blue and green, fiercely rolling.

Breathe

Sit with this experience, as unpleasant as it might be.

Surf

Remember that the physical sensations and feelings you are experiencing are like waves. They come and go. A boat is buffeted by the waves, but it still floats from trough to peak and then down the other side. Likewise, you can remain in the boat and ride this difficult feeling.

Expand

Continue to breathe deeply and slowly. As you breathe, imagine that you are making room for these feelings and sensations. Remember that Christ is with you in your boat. Breathe in and around this difficult feeling and make room for it. Relax around it. Continue doing this until the worst of the feeling or sensation passes. You will notice that the waves have started to dissipate and no longer seem as large as they did before.

Now, instead of only being able to see enormous, threatening waves around you, you can see more of the ocean, and you can gain more perspective about your place in it. Continue to hold this feeling in your awareness and try to connect to your surroundings. Can you hear any sounds? What can you feel against your skin? Open your eyes. What can you see around you?

Refocus

Examine how you feel now. What strength is this painful feeling when you rate it out of ten? Is it different to how you felt at the beginning of this exercise?

Values

In response to this activity, make a choice to do something that is consistent with your faith and values. You might like to reflect on the fact that Jesus is with us always, even when we are feeling overwhelmed or distressed by difficult experiences, just like he was with the disciples in the boat through the storm.

Engage

If it is meaningful to you, say a short prayer. If you decided to follow through with an action or activity, do this now.

MINDFUL ACCEPTANCE OF YOURSELF

For it was you who formed my inward parts;
you knit me together in my mother's womb.
I praise you, for I am fearfully and wonderfully made.
Psalm 139: 13–14

Sometimes one of the hardest things to do is accept our self completely. Knowing that God loves us and we are made in his image can just be head knowledge. Taking the next step and fully accepting this love and the significance of the life we have been given requires a deeper level of peace and grace.

This exercise will help you to accept yourself. You can do this exercise by looking at your face in the mirror or by standing in front of a full-length mirror as your naked self. Choose which of these options you want to try.

MINDFUL ACCEPTANCE OF YOURSELF

Take a moment to really look at yourself.

Look deeply into your eyes. Notice the colour and feeling expressed within them. Look at your face. Look at it as a whole and sit with this image for a moment.

If difficult thoughts or emotions come to mind, notice them with curiosity. Try not to hold on to any one of them, and let them pass naturally. When they come to mind, simply notice them and redirect your focus back to your face.

Go deeper into the exercise by noticing all the individual parts that form your face and all the imperfections that are there, the lines and colour that tell the story of who you are and the life you have lived.

Maybe you have noticed some things you really do not like. If this happens, sit with these feelings, notice they are there and make space for them in your experience. If you need to, breathe deeply in and around them, and try to relax and make room for them. They are part of who you are.

If you have chosen to do the harder version of this task by standing in front of a full-length mirror, follow the same process. This experience will be more intense – most of us have parts of our body we dislike or that our culture tells us should be different or better. When thoughts and feelings about these things come into your mind, allow them to be there and notice them with an attitude of curiosity and acceptance. If you are finding looking at your body confronting, try to make room for any distress or discomfort that you are feeling and continue to look at yourself. Make room for these feelings by breathing into and around them. They will pass in time. It is possible for you to hold these feelings and not be consumed by them. Whenever your mind tries to distract you from the task, redirect your focus to simply looking at your image in the mirror.

Take a moment to reflect on the fact that you have been created in God's image (Gen 1:27). Your worth as a person is not dependent on what you say or do, nor on how you look or dress. You are unique and loved. Nothing can separate us from God's love for us (Rom 8:35–39).

MINDFUL CONNECTION TO GOD'S LOVE

Love is patient; love is kind; love is not envious or boastful or arrogant or rude. It does not insist on its own way; it is not irritable or resentful; it does not rejoice in wrongdoing, but rejoices in the truth. It bears all things, believes all things, hopes all things, endures all things. Love never ends.
1 Corinthians 13:4–8

John's Gospel and letters emphasise one of the main themes of Jesus' message – that God loves us. God is love (1 Jn 4:16). God's character, and therefore Christ's, is the same as the attributes of love that Paul outlines in his first letter to the Corinthians (1 Cor 13:4–8). God has gone to great lengths to demonstrate this love to us by sending his only Son to die on a cross so that we can know God and be forgiven and restore our relationship with him.

The following exercises combine mindful self-compassion, as found in ACT, with the Christian mystic tradition in order to achieve a focus on love and connection with the present. The purpose is to learn to respond to ourselves with grace and acceptance, especially at times when we feel upset, hurt, vulnerable or in pain. It means graciously accepting our faults and weaknesses and embracing the love God freely gives to us.

LET GO OF PAIN

To begin this exercise, close your eyes and sit comfortably in a chair. Bring to mind something that you have been struggling with lately. As you think about this problem, notice all the thoughts and feelings that come into your mind. Think about how this problem is impacting your life – how it has already influenced your past and how it might change the future. Where in your body do you feel most upset when you notice this emotional pain? What does it feel like?

God is always with us. He said he would never leave us or forsake us (Deut 31:6). Imagine he is physically with you now. Imagine he is placing his hand on your pain. If it helps you in this exercise, you might like to place your hand on the place of pain as if it were the Lord's hand comforting you. Imagine that as his hand rests on your pain there is warmth that comes from his love, and the place that hurts is softening around the pain. It is like the pain is lessening its hold on you and his love is allowing you to make room for it.

Sit with this exercise for as long as it is helpful. Ask God to help you with this problem, and prayerfully surrender it to him. Trust that God can help you carry this burden and sustain you.

You might also like to reflect on a Bible passage that is encouraging to you, such as one that speaks about God's love:

Who will separate us from the love of Christ? Will hardship, or distress, or persecution, or famine, or nakedness, or peril, or sword? As it is written,

'For your sake we are being killed all day long;
we are accounted as sheep to be slaughtered.'

No, in all these things we are more than conquerors through him who loved us. For I am convinced that neither death, nor life, nor angels, nor rulers, nor things present, nor things to come, nor powers, nor height, nor depth, nor anything else in all creation, will be able to separate us from the love of God in Christ Jesus our Lord.

Romans 8:35–39

ACCEPT GOD'S GRACE

Close your eyes. Try to bring to mind something you have done, or that has been done to you, where you have felt shame, guilt, regret, anger, sadness or rejection. Remember back to the time when this occurred.

Notice the thoughts that come into your mind, the physical sensations in your body and any feelings you might have. As you do this, try to notice with curiosity, like a young child seeing things for the first time. Do not try to block these thoughts, feelings or urges. Let them be there. Similarly, do not try to engage with, debate with or judge them. Just observe. Try to name these emotions as they arise.

Take a few deep breaths, and imagine that you are making space for these difficult thoughts and feelings as you breathe in and out.

If you need to, ask God to forgive you for your mistake or bad choice. Ask for grace so that you do not repeat it.

Imagine that Christ is sitting with you and that he is extending his love to you. Imagine that he is placing a comforting hand on you and that, as he does this, his kindness, grace and forgiveness flow into you. God is compassionate, gracious and forgiving. Take a moment to accept the gift of grace that is freely given and thank God for it.

> *The LORD is merciful and gracious,*
> *slow to anger and abounding in steadfast love.*
> *He will not always accuse,*
> *nor will he keep his anger for ever.*
> *He does not deal with us according to our sins,*
> *nor repay us according to our iniquities.*
> *For as the heavens are high above the earth,*
> *so great is his steadfast love towards those who fear him;*
> *as far as the east is from the west,*

so far he removes our transgressions from us.
As a father has compassion for his children,
so the LORD has compassion for those who fear him.

Psalm 103:8–13

LIVE A LIFE ROOTED IN GOD[3]

Sit in a quiet place and close your eyes. Reflect on this passage, and as you do, visualise the image of a large tree, with its roots stretched into the ground, its trunk, branches and leaves reaching up into the sky.

Blessed are those who trust in the LORD,
whose trust is the LORD.
They shall be like a tree planted by water,
sending out its roots by the stream.
It shall not fear when heat comes,
and its leaves shall stay green;
in the year of drought it is not anxious,
and it does not cease to bear fruit.

Jeremiah 17:7–8

Plant your feet firmly on the ground. Imagine they are roots that are connected to God, the One who provides living water to you. He sustains you and provides life through this water, no matter how harsh and difficult your surroundings might be.

---

3 Harris, *The Reality Slap*, pp. 38–40.

Then imagine that your body is the trunk of the tree. Place your hands on the lower part of your ribcage. Breathe all of the air slowly out of your lungs until you feel uncomfortable, and then let go, and a reflex will automatically refill your lungs. Repeat this for several deep breaths.

Then extend your focus to your surroundings. Reach out to the world around you like the branches and leaves of a tree extending upwards. Notice what you can see, hear, touch, taste and smell, and then go about your activity fully engaging with everything around you, while keeping an awareness of God's sustaining presence in each moment of your life.

FOCUS ON GOD'S LOVE

Sit quietly and bring to mind one of the Bible passages that speaks of God's love (e.g. Ps 103:8–13; Rom 8:35–9), or focus on a verse of your choice. Read it several times.

In humility, surrender yourself to God and his will and express your love for him. Sit quietly and suspend your rational mind with all its thoughts. Focus on God.

When you become distracted, gently redirect your thoughts back to God. Try to continue this silence for several minutes, and in the quietness open yourself to God's Spirit.

9

The Sensory Realm

hese exercises use the five senses to connect with the present moment. Although they do not strictly fall within either ACT or Christian contemplative prayer tradition, they use the same idea to pay attention to what is happening in the now.

MINDFUL BODY AWARENESS

So God created humankind in his image,
in the image of God he created them;
male and female he created them.
Genesis 1:27

Our entire body is a reminder that we were created in God's image. It is a great resource for exploring the wonder of God as Creator and our identity – ranging from the uniqueness of our individual fingerprints through to an acceptance of who we are and how we look. God created only one person like us, and this makes us unique and special.

MINDFUL AWARENESS OF YOUR FINGERPRINT

Look at your finger, starting with the top side. Look at the colour of the skin, the shape of your fingernail. What does it look like?

Gently run your other hand over the tip of this finger, and feel the different texture of your nail compared to your skin around it. What is the difference? Is there also a difference in colour between these two parts? How many different colours are there on your fingernail? Can you see the moon shape at the base? How prominent is it? If you write with this hand, can you see any signs of wear where you hold a pen to write? Has writing affected the shape or condition of the skin?

Now turn your finger over. Look closely at the pattern of your fingerprint. This is unique to you. No one else has a print quite like it. When you touch this part of your finger to another on your hand, what sensation do you feel? What does the skin on this finger feel like? Now look more closely at your finger. Can you find any scars? Do the joints show signs of arthritis? Is it straight or crooked? Is there any discolouration?

Take a moment to reflect on the fact that God created you in his image. We have the fingerprint of God on our life. God created you and cares for you, and he knows everything about you.

MINDFUL CONNECTION TO YOUR BODY

Are not two sparrows sold for a penny? Yet not one of them will fall to the ground unperceived by your Father. And even the hairs of your head are all counted. So do not be afraid; you are of more value than many sparrows.
Matthew 10: 29–31

This is a helpful exercise to increase your awareness of what is going on in your body. It is particularly helpful for people suffering stress or anxiety, or an illness that has an aspect of pain or discomfort, as many of these physical conditions cause tension and distress. Often over time we become disconnected to how they are impacting the functioning of our body. Increased awareness can help us towards a greater level of self-care.

MINDFUL CONNECTION TO YOUR BODY – SHORT FORM

Get yourself into a comfortable position, either sitting or lying down. Use your observing self to focus on your body. During this exercise, when thoughts come into your awareness, let them pass through your mind and simply return your focus to your body. Observe what is happening.

Start with your breathing. Is it fast or slow, shallow or deep? If you notice you are breathing quickly, or from the top of your chest, redirect your breath so it is filling all of your lungs. You can check this by placing your hands on the bottom of your rib cage. Breathe slowly and deeply.

Examine your head. What sensations can you feel? Is your jaw tight? Are there areas that hurt? If there are areas in your face that are tense, try to completely relax them. Take a deep breath, and as you exhale let the tension go. Do the same with your neck and shoulders. Consciously relax any muscles that are tense. Breathe deeply and let it go.

Now focus on the rest of your body. Are there any areas that are hot or cold? Do you have any prickling, aching or other uncomfortable sensations? Where are they and what do they feel like? Observe these feelings and sensations with curiosity and openness. If you can find areas of pain, consciously try to relax the area around it. Make space for this feeling and accept its presence.

Is your body straight or leaning to one side? If your spine or arms, legs or head are crooked, change your position so they are straight again. Notice whether you have any urges to move or change position, or a wish to avoid this exercise. Notice the presence of these feelings and accept them.

Continue this exercise for several minutes.

MINDFUL CONNECTION TO YOUR BODY – EXTENDED VERSION

Close your eyes and take a moment to focus quietly on the sounds you can hear around you. Then bring your focus further into your body and notice the rise and fall of your chest as you breathe in and out. Keep doing this until your mind is quiet and still.

Then focus your attention on your face and head. See if you can feel any muscle tension in these areas. If you do, let it go so that the muscles in these areas are completely relaxed and floppy. It is sometimes easiest to relax your muscles as you breathe out (just like when you do a muscle stretch).

Next, focus on your neck. Do the same thing as before, noticing if there is any tension, and then release and relax the muscles in this area. Now go back and notice your face, head and neck, and try and keep all three areas relaxed at the same time.

Now focus on your shoulders. Let your shoulder blades slide down your back and straighten slightly so you can relax this area. Then do the same as before and revisit your face, head, neck and shoulders and keep all these areas relaxed at the same time.

Use the same process to focus on and relax your arms and hands, and once again revisit the areas you have already relaxed.

The trunk of your body – your chest, stomach and back – is the next part to pay attention to. This time notice the rhythm and speed and depth of your breathing. It has probably changed and become slower than when you started. You are starting to relax.

The last areas to release are your legs and feet. You might need to move these parts of your body to relax them. Get them into the most comfortable position you can find. Then, revisit your whole body and make sure all your muscles are completely relaxed.

You can stay in these exercises for a while, continuing to focus on your body and breathing deeply. When the time comes to end the exercise, gradually bring yourself back into your surroundings. First, focus on the sounds you can hear around you. Then open your eyes and adjust to the light and the space around you.

MINDFUL COLOURING

In the beginning when God created the heavens and the earth, the earth was a formless void and darkness covered the face of the deep, while a wind from God swept over the face of the waters. Then God said, 'Let there be light'; and there was light. God saw that the light was good; and God separated the light from the darkness.

Genesis 1:1–4

We enjoy light and colour through our visual sense. Mindful colouring can be one way of applying this appreciation. Even though colouring books are popular, few of these books explain how to practise connecting with the present while you are doing this task. Colouring does not require rational thinking, and therefore this task can take on a meditative quality that purely uses the observing self. This is why most people tend to find it relaxing.

The process is simple. As with the other exercises, settle in a quiet place, in a comfortable position and free of other distractions. Then select the page you wish to colour. If you want to use this task to focus on God, you might like to choose a Celtic cross design. Alternatively, you might wish to create your own unique colouring page and print it out (there are numerous software programs that help you do this)[1] or use an app on your phone or other touchscreen device to colour in designs electronically.

COLOURING BETWEEN THE LINES

When you are ready and have all your materials in place, focus on observing. Look at the colours available, choose one and focus on observing how the pencil feels in your hand. Watch the pencil move over the page and between the lines. Notice it move up and down on the page. Watch the texture and colour that is created. Move to your next colour. Try to do this simply by observing and focusing on the process. When you get distracted and notice your mind is drifting to memories or thoughts of the day, gently redirect your focus to the task at hand. Continue to do this until you have completed your design.

A MUSTARD SEED

He put before them another parable: 'The kingdom of heaven is like a mustard seed that someone took and sowed in his field; it is the smallest of all the seeds, but when it has grown it is the greatest of shrubs and becomes a tree, so that the birds of the air come and make nests its branches.'
Matthew 13:31–32

---

1 For example, *Colorfly* or *Pigment*.

Eating is a sensory experience. The pleasure of eating is about what the food looks like, what it smells like, and the taste and texture it has when it is in your mouth. Mindful eating forces us to slow down and take in all of the experience and become aware of this process. This exercise takes conventional mindful eating and extends it to inspire reflection on our faith – by using a mustard seed. You could also try this with foods used in other biblical metaphors and parables, such as salt, yeast or bread.

MINDFUL REFLECTION ON A MUSTARD SEED

Hold a mustard seed in your hand. Look at it closely. What colour is it? Look at the texture, size and shape.

Try running your finger gently over the external surface? What does it feel like when you roll it across your palm with your finger? Try holding it between two fingers and take a closer look.

Bring the mustard seed up to your nose. Can you smell any aroma? What is it like?

Hold the mustard seed up to your mouth and then slowly place it inside. What is happening now? As you do this, try not to chew or swallow yet. Take the time to feel the seed with your tongue. What does it taste like? What texture can you feel on your tongue?

Now when you are ready, start to slowly chew it. Notice what is happening inside your mouth. Does the texture or taste change as you continue to eat it? When you are ready, swallow.

Your mind will try to distract you with other thoughts and feelings, rather than slowing down to observe the process. When this happens, gently redirect your attention to connecting with your experience and focusing on the seed.

As you finish the task, take a moment to reflect on Jesus' parable about the mustard seed. Allow the Holy Spirit to speak to you in the silence. End this exercise with a mental prayer as you feel led.

MINDFUL EATING - A WHOLE MEAL

Jesus said to them, 'I am the bread of life. Whoever comes to me will never be hungry, and whoever believes in me will never be thirsty.'
John 6:35

Therefore do not worry, saying, 'What will we eat?' or 'What will we drink?' or 'What will we wear?' For it is the Gentiles who strive for all these things; and indeed your heavenly Father knows that you need all these things. But strive first for the kingdom of God and his righteousness, and all these things will be given to you as well.
Matthew 6:31–33

This exercise is for use during meals. Instead of mindlessly eating quickly, why not focus, slow down and enjoy the experience? Eating slowly gives your body time to digest food and register how full you are. You can do this task during any meal, either alone or with your family or friends.

MINDFUL EATING

Before you start eating, take the time to look at the presentation of what is before you. Take in the colours, textures and shapes. Smell the aroma. If it is hot, feel the steam on your face.

Take a moment to thank God for providing for your daily needs.

With a grateful attitude, think about the things that have been provided for you, your family and friends.

You might like to light a candle at the centre of the table to represent God's presence with you during your meal.

As you eat, fully connect with the experience. Notice the texture and taste of each bite of food. How does it feel in your mouth? What smells and tastes can you notice? Is the food chewy, smooth or melting in your mouth? What reaction do these sensations cause within you? Are they triggering thoughts, feelings or memories? If they are, notice these and then gently redirect your focus back to your meal and what is happening at the table around you.

If you are with other people, what are they talking about? What is their emotional expression? Try to fully engage in conversation with them. Mindfully listen with an attitude of compassion, grace and acceptance, putting aside your own needs and agenda. Enjoy this time of intense sensory experience and connection to others with an attitude of gratitude to God.

MINDFUL LISTENING

By wisdom a house is built,
and by understanding it is established;
by knowledge the rooms are filled
with all precious and pleasant riches.
Proverbs 24:3–4

Mindful listening is a great way to improve your listening skills so that you learn to immerse yourself in the experience of another person. Often when we talk to people we care about we spend much of the time distracted, thinking about something else or what we want to say next. Or, we get caught up in our reaction to what the other person is saying. We might feel angry or stressed about the interaction. As these things are happening to us on the inside, we are limiting our ability to tune in to the other person.

To really listen, we need to be able to enter our friend's world. We need to hear what they are saying, but also see how they feel, understand what is important to them and understand their perspective. To do this well, we need to reduce the influence of our rational or reactive mind and use our observing mind to bring awareness to the other person.

You might like to practise mindful listening by putting time aside to have coffee with your partner or friend, or while talking to your child at the kitchen table. You could choose to go for a walk with another person and practise silent listening. It does not matter where you practise this activity. Try to do this for at least five to ten minutes to start with. It is important that you bring to this exercise an attitude of acceptance of the other person and their experience, focusing on them without being drawn into responding verbally. Stay silent, and provide encouragement through your body language and eye contact.

For spouses and partners who wish to practise this task regularly, you might find it helpful to choose a topic to use as the focus of the listening task – for example, a special memory, a significant life event, or a worry, concern or problem. Do this task, and then swap roles and continue.

As with all the other mindfulness tasks discussed so far, you might find it hard to stay silent and listen at the beginning because it feels unnatural. You might find it awkward, or notice you have been dragged away from listening by your own thoughts and emotions. Persevere. This is a skill that you get better at with practice. The reward will be a deeper understanding and acceptance of the other person, and they will feel valued and listened to.

MINDFUL LISTENING TO ANOTHER PERSON

Observe the expression on the other person's face. Look into their eyes. Notice their body language. Observe their emotions. How does their voice sound? Are they talking softly, or are they loud and animated? Is their speech calm and slow, or is it fast? Are they acting in a relaxed way, or are they stressed or emotional?

Be mindful about your own reactions and feelings to this conversation. Notice the feelings and thoughts that are trying to distract you from focusing on the other person. When your mind tries to drag you away from listening, be aware of the story that is causing this and then gently refocus on listening. If you find yourself being buffeted by waves of emotion, let them be there. If necessary, take a few deep breaths and then gently refocus on listening to the other person.

Mindful listening can also be done individually, by connecting to sounds you can hear around you or by listening to music.

MINDFUL LISTENING IN NATURE

Take a moment to go outside. Sit down and close your eyes. Try to relax and observe the sounds around you. Do this for five minutes. When you notice your rational mind cutting in and distracting you, gently redirect your focus back to listening.

MINDFUL LISTENING TO MUSIC

Choose a piece of classical music and sit quietly to listen to it. Alternatively, you might like to lie on your bed and listen with your headphones in. Fully observe all the different sounds you can hear. If you start to get distracted, gently redirect your focus to just listening to the music.

If classical music is not your natural preference, you might like to choose another song or piece of music that you like. You can make this task God focused by selecting music that is consistent with this theme. Fully engage with listening. Focus completely on the music. As before, do not be surprised by distractions. When they occur, notice them, then focus again on observing.

10

Contemplative Connection to the Now

U p to this point we have been connecting to our self and the present moment by using our five senses and some techniques from ACT. This chapter builds on these techniques, showing how we can use them to facilitate our moment-to-moment connection to God.

MINDFUL FOCUS ON GOD THROUGHOUT OUR DAY

Am I now seeking human approval, or God's approval? Or am I trying to please people? If I were still pleasing people, I would not be a servant of Christ.

Galatians 1:10

Slaves, obey your earthly masters with fear and trembling, in singleness of heart, as you obey Christ; not only while being watched, and in order to please them, but as slaves of Christ, doing the will of God from the heart. Render service with enthusiasm, as to the Lord and not to men and women.

Ephesians 6:5–7

Brother Lawrence continually practised being in God's presence.[1] Every thought and action was directed by his love for God and his awareness of God's presence with him. The way he lived was like a

1 Brother Lawrence, *The Practice of the Presence of God.*

seamless prayer that began when he woke in the morning and ended when he went to bed in the evening. This was only possible by cultivating an open and accepting attitude that was God focused and which deeply connected the present moment with his faith.

Brother Lawrence challenges us to live with a similar attitude that practises the presence of God in everything we do. He based his attitude on the two Bible passages above.

PRACTISING THE PRESENCE OF GOD

Start your day by reflecting on Galatians 1:10 and Ephesians 6:5–7. Try to do everything mindfully and prayerfully with a servant heart that is motivated by pleasing God.

Then say the following prayer:

> O my God, since you are with me, and I must now, in obedience to your commands, apply my mind to these outward things, I ask you to grant me the grace to continue in your Presence; and to this end prosper me with your assistance, receive all my works, and possess all my affections.[2]

As you go about your daily tasks, continually converse with God. Ask for grace to serve, and offer God all of your actions.

When you reach the end of your day, examine yourself and consider how you did your work. If it went well, give praise to God. If you feel you could have done better, ask forgiveness. But be careful not to dwell on your mistakes, because this will distract you from focusing on the presence of God.

---

2 Brother Lawrence, *The Practice of the Presence of God*, p. 246.

MINDFUL CONNECTION TO BREATH WITH A FOCUS ON WORDS

But Moses said to God, 'If I come to the Israelites and say to them, "The God of your ancestors has sent me to you", and they ask me, "What is his name?" what shall I say to them?' God said to Moses, 'I AM WHO I AM.'
Exodus 3:13–14

The following exercise is adapted from a meditation exercise found in Richard Rohr's book, *The Naked Now*.[3] In Jewish tradition, the name Yahweh was not spoken aloud as this name for God was held in such high esteem. In Exodus 20:7 it says, 'Do not utter the name of God in vain' (NIV). God's name was to be held in reverence and awe.

While this word was not spoken, it was breathed. The name contains two syllables. When whispered it resembles the sound of inhaling and exhaling. It can be spoken in time with breathing. *Yah* is the inhalation and *weh* the exhalation.

This Jewish tradition can be used as a type of meditative prayer in conjunction with rhythmic breathing. Breathing connects us to God. Breath is the thing that gives us life, and it also represents the work of the Holy Spirit, as seen when Christ breathed on the disciples (Jn 20:21).

RHYTHMIC BREATHING WHILE FOCUSING ON ONE WORD

Seat yourself in a comfortable position in a quiet place where there are no distractions. Shut your eyes and gently bring your attention to the rise and fall of your breath. Do not try to alter your breathing. Just notice it with curiosity and concentrate on it.

---

3 Rohr, *The Naked Now*.

Take several slow, deep breaths. Then bring your awareness to intentionally focus on the word Yahweh. As you breathe in, say the first syllable, 'yah'. Then as you breathe out, say the second syllable, 'weh'. Continue to do this for several minutes, or for as long as you are able. If you become distracted, gently redirect your focus to the rhythmic repetition of God's name.

MINDFUL CONNECTION TO BREATH AS A WALKING MEDITATION

Your word is a lamp for my feet a light on my path.
Psalm 119:105

This next exercise was inspired by an exercise out of Richard Rohr's book, *The Naked Now*.[4] He discovered that in walking up stairs, it is possible to train the breath so that you inhale and exhale in time with each step. As he did this, he found that he was saying two words as he went: in – 'beauty', out – 'back'. On reflection, he found that these words, beauty and back, were out of one of his favourite Christian poems. Put together, they referred to giving beauty back.

WALKING MEDITATION

Try going out for a walk and focusing your mind on two words that are meaningful to you. Using breath awareness, breathe one word on the inhalation, and the other on the exhalation.

---

4 Rohr, *The Naked Now*.

This exercise can be done anywhere, but it might be easiest when walking up a steep hill or up and down stairs, so that your steps are rhythmic and allow for focused breathing. You might also try walking a labyrinth if one is available to you.

Suggested words might be:

Lamp + feet (Ps 119:105)

Feet + rock (Ps 40:2)

Good + news (Isa 52:7)

Path + righteousness (Ps 23:3)

Path + peace (Lk 1:79)

Step + Spirit (Gal 5:25)

EXPLORING ASPECTS OF PRAYER

This exercise is based upon the work of St Teresa of Avila[5] and blends contemplative prayer and mindful connection to your thoughts and feelings.

JOURNEY WITHIN A MANSION

Find a place free of distractions to sit quietly for several minutes. Close your eyes. Imagine you are standing outside a large house or mansion. Outside this house are a whole lot of noisy and moving creatures. One type of creature is the busy part of your mind – the rational part of your thinking. In this

---

5 Teresa of Avila, *Interior Castle.*

place you are constantly bombarded by thoughts that come in the form of worries, fears, memories, judgements and distractions. Another type of creature is your emotions. They come in a stream of different feelings, accompanied by a range of bodily sensations and urges. Sit quietly, and let these things come to your awareness. What thoughts, feelings and urges do you notice? Are there themes in these thoughts? Take a moment to name each one as you notice them.

You might like to take a moment to reflect. You could:

1. write your thoughts and feelings in a journal.

2. make a list of things that you are worrying about.

3. draw a picture that represents how you feel.

4. simply notice what is happening in your mind and body now.

5. reflect on what has been happening up to this point of your day or week.

Then enter the front door of the mansion. Take a moment to bring these things before God in prayer. Name each thought, feeling or urge that is bothering you. Ask God to help direct your thoughts.

Surrender any worries or fears to him. Spend a few minutes in mental prayer, conversing with God.

Next, imagine you are walking through the second door of this mansion. As you do, you move further away from the distractions outside. You are standing in a white, empty room with two doors. As your thoughts and feelings and urges come to you, let them enter through the door on the left and exit through the door on the right. Notice them. You might like to label them: for example, 'worry'. Do not get caught up in these thoughts, feelings and urges. Just notice them. Let them come in, pass through and exit. Try to keep your focus on the room.

Go further into the mansion. Redirect your focus from yourself to God. Then, light a candle to represent God's presence with you. Focus on this light and on God. Spend some time sitting in silence with your will completely surrendered to God. Have an attitude of listening as you sit in God's presence, and allow God's Spirit to speak to you.

Finally, prepare yourself for life outside this mansion. As you leave this mental space, use all your senses to reconnect to what is happening around you. Notice what you can see, hear, taste, smell and touch. Orient your mind towards the rest of the day and the tasks that lie before you. Ask Christ to be in your thoughts and actions as you go about your activities.

MERTON-INSPIRED CONTEMPLATION

There is no such thing as a kind of prayer in which you do absolutely nothing ... contemplative prayer is a deep and simplified spiritual activity in which the mind and will rest in a unified and simple concentration upon God, turned to him, intent upon him and absorbed in his own light, with a simple gaze which is perfect adoration because it silently tells God that we have left everything else and desire even to leave our own selves for his sake, and that He alone is important to us, He alone is our desire and our life, and nothing else can give us any joy.[6]

Contemplative prayer is essentially like connecting to the present moment, except here you are connecting in the present moment to God. If you are struggling to sit in contemplative prayer and focus yourself on God, try using one of these ideas to get you started.

FOCUS ON A PASSAGE OF THE BIBLE OR A BOOK ABOUT YOUR FAITH

Start your prayer time by reading a passage in the Bible or another book. Ask God to speak to you through the words that you read. When you reach a word, phrase, concept or idea that stands out to you, stop. Focus on this one thing meditatively. Ask God's Spirit to speak to you. As you focus, your thoughts and feelings will try to distract you. When this happens, gently redirect your attention to what you were focusing on. Continue with this activity for as long as you are able. Finish your time of contemplation with a short mental prayer of thanks to God.

FOCUS ON A PIECE OF RELIGIOUS ART OR AN OBJECT

For this contemplation, find a visual image that has religious meaning. You could choose an icon, a painting, a photograph or a sculpture. You could also try tangible objects that

---

6 Merton, *New Seeds of Contemplation*, p. 243.

are meaningful, like a small wooden cross, a mustard seed, some water, bread, blades of grass, or a fig.

Start by looking intently at the image or object. Use your observing self and your five senses to take all the details in. Consider what the artist was trying to say. Does this image or form impact you in some way? How does it focus your attention on God? What inspiration and meaning can you draw from it? Focus your attention to connecting to a specific aspect of this artwork or object. Use it to help you connect with and focus on an aspect of God.

Continue with this activity for as long as you are able. Finish your time of contemplation with a short mental prayer to God in response to your meditation.

FOCUS ON CREATION

Intentionally go out into creation and contemplate the landscape in front of you. Sit silently in your surroundings and bring a simple awareness of God's presence through creation.

Observe the natural environment around you and consider the details that you would not normally notice. Use your five senses to do this. Contemplate God as Creator of all that you see.

Continue with this activity for as long as you are able. As the Psalmists did, let your time of connecting with God's world finish with a mental prayer of praise and thanksgiving for all that is around you and for the God who created it.

HEARING GOD IN SCRIPTURE

Dallas Willard has brought *lectio divina* exercises back into mainstream Christian practice.[7] This form of Christian meditation focuses on Scripture, allowing God's Spirit to speak through the repeated reading, silent reflection on and application of the passage.

LECTIO DIVINA

You can use any passage from the Bible. Psalm 23 is used here as an example.

> The LORD is my shepherd, I shall not want.
> He makes me lie down in green pastures;
> he leads me beside still waters;
> he restores my soul.
> He leads me in right paths
> for his name's sake.
> Even though I walk through the darkest valley,
> I fear no evil;
> for you are with me;
> your rod and your staff –
> they comfort me.
> You prepare a table before me
> in the presence of my enemies;
> you anoint my head with oil;
> my cup overflows.
> Surely goodness and mercy shall follow me

---

7 Willard, *Hearing God*, pp. 48–51.

all the days of my life,
and I shall dwell in the house of the LORD
my whole life long.

Ask God to speak to you through the following exercise.

Read ('lectio')

Read the passage slowly. Then read the passage a second time, remembering that the people in the text would have experienced the events just like we would if we were in their place. As you read, listen for a word, phrase, character or part of the story that stands out to you. Try not to choose this yourself. Instead, let God's Spirit bring it to your attention.

Reflect ('meditatio')

Read the passage again slowly. While you do so, reflect on the part that came to your attention. Think about why this word, phrase, character or idea stood out to you. What draws you to this word, phrase or idea? How does it feel to be like this person? How does it make you feel and think about yourself or God? Pray and ask God to show you how this applies to your life today.

Respond in prayer ('oratio')

Read the passage one last time. As you do, pray to God about what you think the Spirit is saying to you. You might respond with a prayer of thanks or request.

Rest and contemplate ('contemplatio')

Follow where you feel led in this exercise. You could sit in silence and be with God. You might focus specifically on an aspect of God. This might be from the passage you read. Simply sit and immerse yourself in your relationship with God.

A TASTE OF IGNATIUS

In his *Spiritual Exercises*, Ignatius of Loyola encourages us to use our five senses, and our feelings and thoughts, to fully focus on one scene or story from the life of Jesus.[8] This meditation has been adapted from the original version used by Ignatius and presented in updated form. It is based on the nativity.

THE NATIVITY

Say a prayer of thanksgiving

Read Luke 2:1–20.

Try to fully imagine this scene in your mind. Consider the long journey that Mary and Joseph made to Bethlehem. Consider what it was like for the shepherds to see the angels in the sky, speaking to them and praising God. Consider what it was like for the shepherds to stumble into the birth of Jesus, who was lying in a manger, surrounded by Mary and Joseph. Imagine what this scene would look like – the sounds, smells and physical feelings. To connect to this scene in the present, use your five senses and your imagination.

---

8 St Ignatius of Loyola, *The Spiritual Exercises*.

Reflect on how Christ was born in poverty at the end of a long journey. His parents were hungry, thirsty and tired. Think about how this was the start of a longer journey that was to end with him dying on the cross for you.

Consider the shepherds in the fields and the words the angels spoke to them: 'Do not be afraid; for see – I am bringing good news of great joy for all the people: to you is born this day in the city of David a Saviour, who is the Messiah, the Lord' (Lk 2:10–11); 'Glory to God in the highest, and on earth peace among those whom he favours!' (Lk 2:14).

Ask God to teach you something about this passage so that you can know more about Christ and serve and follow him.

Think about how this passage applies to you serving Jesus as the King eternal. As a subject and servant of the King, how do you wish to respond to this passage?

Say a mental prayer to ask for knowledge about Christ, who became human for us. Ask that you might love and follow him more greatly than you do now.

End with a prayer of praise.

You can adapt this contemplation exercise by substituting other passages from the life of Jesus as contained in the Gospels. You can try visualising parables instead of narrative passages. Sitting in an environment that relates to the story you are focusing on may assist you to use your senses. For example, meditating on John 15, the passage about the vine and the branches, can be enriched by sitting in front of a grapevine and examining it closely to bring the metaphor to life.

THREE METHODS OF CONTEMPLATIVE PRAYER

These three methods of prayer have been adapted from St Ignatius's *Spiritual Exercises.*[9]

CONTEMPLATIVE PRAYER – METHOD 1

In the *Spiritual Exercises*, we are encouraged to reflect on the Ten Commandments, the deadly sins, the powers of the soul and the way we use our five senses. As an example, this exercise focuses on the fruit of the Spirit, Galatians 5:22–23. You could also use the characteristics of love in 1 Corinthians 13:4–8.

To begin with, say a prayer of thanksgiving.

Then read Galatians 5:22–23: 'By contrast, the fruit of the Spirit is love, joy, peace, patience, kindness, generosity, faithfulness, gentleness, and self-control. There is no law against such things.'

Ask for the grace of God to know where you have fallen short in showing the fruit of the Spirit in your life this week. Ask for a better understanding of what these fruits are, and how God has transformed your life so that you have these characteristics.

Consider each characteristic – how you have shown it in your life and how you have failed to do so. If you find fault in yourself, ask forgiveness.

Offer a prayer of praise to God.

---

9 St Ignatius of Loyola, *The Spiritual Exercises*, Three Methods of Prayer.

CONTEMPLATIVE PRAYER – METHOD 2

The second method of prayer in *The Spiritual Exercises* contemplates the meaning of just one word.[10] This is similar to the type of meditative prayers contained in *The Cloud of Unknowing*.[11] You might like to choose one of the following words to meditate upon: love, life, light, Spirit, God, Christ, Creator, Abba or Father. Alternatively, use a word or phrase of your choice from the Bible or a traditional prayer. The purpose of this contemplation is to help you focus your attention, with love, on God.

Begin by a mental prayer of thanksgiving.

Kneel, sit or walk depending on what is most comfortable. Close your eyes or fix them on one place.

Focus your attention on the one word you have chosen.

When you do this exercise, your mind will wander. When it does, gently bring your focus back onto this one word.

Continue for as long as you are able or until you have reached the end of the prayer you are reciting.

End by asking God to make you more like Christ.

CONTEMPLATIVE PRAYER – METHOD 3

The third method of prayer in the *Spiritual Exercises* is done by rhythm.[12] You can use just one word, as with method 2, or

---

10 Ibid.
11 Unknown, *The Cloud of Unknowing*.
12 St Ignatius of Loyola, *The Spiritual Exercises*, Three Methods of Prayer.

you can use a traditional prayer, like St Patrick's Breastplate,[13] and pray through it one word at a time. Again, the purpose of this contemplation is to help you focus your attention, with love, on God.

> Christ with me,
>
> Christ before me,
>
> Christ behind me,
>
> Christ in me,
>
> Christ beneath me,
>
> Christ above me,
>
> Christ on my right,
>
> Christ on my left,
>
> Christ when I lie down,
>
> Christ when I sit down,
>
> Christ when I arise,
>
> Christ in the heart of every man who thinks of me,
>
> Christ in the mouth of everyone who speaks of me,
>
> Christ in every eye that sees me,
>
> Christ in every ear that hears me.

First, say a mental prayer of thanksgiving.

Kneel, sit or walk depending on what is most comfortable. Close your eyes or fix them on one place.

With each breath in or out, say one word, or one word of a prayer, in rhythm with these breaths.

In the space between breaths, let your attention be on the meaning of the word spoken.

---

13 St Patrick, *St. Patrick's Breastplate.*

When you do this exercise, your mind will wander. When it does, gently bring your focus back onto this one word.

Continue for as long as you are able, or until you have reached the end of the prayer you are reciting.

End by asking God to make you more like Christ.

SHARED COMMUNITY CONNECTION WITH CHRIST

Christians actively practise a form of individual and collective contemplation at Advent and Christmas, as well as Lent and Easter. We remember the birth of Jesus and his death and resurrection. We also regularly remember Jesus' death on the cross and resurrection each time we celebrate communion or mass. Thomas Merton encourages us to not only practise individual contemplation, but to extend this to a shared experience in these events.[14]

The following variation of the Lord's Supper has been written so that a group of people can contemplate Jesus' death and resurrection together. It intentionally goes deeper into the contemplative method than the forms of mental prayer usually experienced during communion within a church service. This exercise requires one person to direct the group in this corporate contemplation. The prayers and blessing in this exercise have been taken from *Common Prayer: A Liturgy for Ordinary Radicals*.[15]

---

14 Merton, *New Seeds of Contemplation*.
15 Claiborne, Wilson-Hartgrove & Okoro, *Common Prayer*, p. 564.

THE DEATH AND RESURRECTION OF CHRIST

Set the scene

Choose a piece of music that will provide focus on the death and resurrection of Christ. Sing or listen to this song together.

Provide a point of focus, such as a candle representing the light and presence of Christ or a cross symbolising his death and resurrection.

See and imagine 1

Leader:

Listen to the passage about Jesus' death on the cross.

Imagine yourself as an onlooker of the scene as it is unfolding. The crowd who followed Jesus, the crucifixion of Jesus with the two criminals, the darkness and Jesus' death, and the reaction and the dissipation of the crowds after he died.

Focus your mind on the image of Jesus on the cross. Focus your attention on this one thing with an attitude of openness to God.

Read Luke 23:26–49.

Reflect on your own thoughts and behaviour over the past week, and connect with the reason for why Jesus died for you and all the world.

See and imagine 2

Leader:

Listen to the passage about the resurrection of Christ.

Imagine yourself as an onlooker to the events of the resurrection. The women arriving at the tomb to find the body had disappeared, the angels telling them that Jesus had risen and has gone, the women telling the apostles about what they had seen, and Peter running to the tomb to see for himself.

Focus your mind on the image of the empty tomb with an attitude of openness to God.

Read Luke 24:1–12.

Reflect on what the resurrection means to your life and the significance of the transformative presence of the Holy Spirit.

Corporate prayer of thanksgiving

Leader:

'The table of bread is now to be made ready.
It is the table of company with Jesus,
And all who love him.
It is the table of sharing with the poor of the world,
With whom Jesus identified himself.
It is the table of communion with the earth,
In which Christ became incarnate.
So come to this table,
You who have much faith
And you who would like to have more;
You who have been here often
And you who have not been for a long time;

You who have tried to follow Jesus,

And you who have failed;

Come.

It is Christ who invites us to meet him here.'[16]

All:

'Loving God,

through your goodness

we have this bread and wine/grape juice to offer,

which has come forth from the earth

and human hands have made.

May we know your presence in the sharing

so that we may know your touch

and presence in all things.

We celebrate the life that Jesus has shared

among his community through the centuries,

and shares with us now.

Made one in Christ

and one with each other,

we offer these gifts and with them ourselves,

a single, living act of praise.

Amen.'[17]

Serve the bread and the wine/juice. Share these together in silent reflection.

---

16 Ibid., p. 564.
17 Ibid.

Blessing

Leader:

'May the peace of the Lord Christ go with you: wherever he may send you; may he guide you through the wilderness: protect you through the storm may he bring you home rejoicing: at the wonders he has shown you'[18]

---

18 Ibid.

Conclusion
Next Steps

This book has taken us on a journey that started with a whole range of questions about whether followers of Christ should engage in mindfulness meditation. We have systematically answered these and discovered that most mindfulness mediation is based on Buddhist religious practices and has been separated from its original context and placed within therapy. These therapies do result in measurable changes, such as improved mental health, reduced physical stress and improvements in focused attention and mood. But the science that backs them up needs improvement and replication.

We have grappled with the idea of whether mindfulness is consistent with Christian faith and if it should be separated from its religious origin. I have argued that we need to be discerning and not just incorporate it without thinking into our daily life, as everything we spend time doing works to change our brain for good or ill. The changes we make to our mind need to be based on our values and beliefs in order to create lasting inner transformation. We do not want to open ourselves up to a practice that takes us away from God or opens us up to harmful spiritual influences. Acceptance and commitment therapy offers one alternative way we can connect with the now and apply this to our faith values in order to create lasting change without relying on Buddhist mindfulness meditation.

We have walked a path of discovery through the Christian tradition, starting with Scripture and early forms of Christian mysticism, and ending with contemporary teaching on contemplative prayer. This provides us with a biblical framework to understand meditation and connection to God. We kept coming back to the ideas of abiding with Christ in the image of the vine, and in God's Spirit breathing life and transformation into our spirit and life. We were challenged that the central aspect to connecting to God and our self simultaneously required surrender of our will and a continual attitude of love towards God. This rich tradition provides a faith-based alternative to Buddhist mindfulness that allows God's Spirit to create change in our life.

We have found that Christ-centred mindfulness means holistic transformation so that we have the mind of Christ. We become connected to our self and to God moment to moment, in the now.

I have offered a range of different ways you can practise this form of connecting to self and God. As a next step, I would encourage you to build a regular form and attitude of Christ-centred mindfulness into your day. You could do this in the following ways:

- Take a moment to stop and focus simply on what you can see, hear, touch, taste and smell. As you do, hold an attitude of gratitude and openness to God.
- Connect more fully to what your family members are saying and the tasks you do by undertaking these actions as if you were doing them for Christ.
- Add silent prayer into your regular mental prayer time.

- Bring Scripture to life by using your imagination or by repeating the reading and asking God to direct your thoughts.
- Try doing these things with a friend or as part of a Bible study group.

Be creative. The exercises in this book are just a start. You can adapt your own, and do them anywhere and with anyone.

And this is my prayer, that your love may overflow more and more
with knowledge and full insight to help you determine what is best,
so that on the day of Christ you may be pure and blameless, having
produced the harvest of righteousness that comes through Jesus Christ
for the glory and praise of God.

Philippians 1:9–11

Bibliography

Brother Lawrence. *The Practice of the Presence of God: The Best Rule of Holy Life*, in *Top 7 Catholic Classics: On Loving God, The Cloud of Unknowing, Dialogue of Saint Catherine of Siena, The Imitation of Christ, Interior Castle, Dark Night of the Soul, The Practice of the Presence of God* (Top Christian Classics Book 3), Amazon Digital Services, London, 2012, Kindle edition.

Butler, T.C. *Word Biblical Commentary Joshua 1–12*, Zondervan, Grand Rapids MI, 2014.

Chiesa, A. and Malinowski, P. 'Mindfulness-based approaches: are they all the same?', *Journal of Clinical Psychology*, vol. 67, no. 4, 2011, pp. 404–24.

Claiborne, S., Wilson-Hartgrove, J. and Okoro, E. *Common Prayer: A Liturgy for Ordinary Radicals*, Zondervan, Grand Rapids MI, 2010.

Craigie, P.C. Word Biblical Commentary Psalms 1–50 (Vol. 19), Word Books, Waco TX, 1983.

Dawson, G. and Turnbull, L. 'Is mindfulness the new optiate of the masses? Critical reflections from a Buddhist perspective', *Psychotherapy*, vol. 12, no. 4, 2006, pp. 60–64.

Doidge, N. *The Brain That Changes Itself*, Penguin Books, New York, 2007.

Doney, M. *Discovering Our World*, Lion Publishing, Ipswich UK, 1979.

Dunn, J.D.G. *Word Biblical Commentary Romans 1–8* (vol. 38), Word Books, Dallas TX, 1988.

Fjorback, L.O., Arendt, M., Ornbol, E., Fink, P. and Walach, H. 'Mindfulness-based stress reduction and mindfulness-based cognitive therapy: a systematic review of randomized controlled trials', *Acta Psychiatrica Scandanavica*, vol. 124, 2011, pp. 102–19.

Forsyth, J.P. and Eifert, G.H. *The Mindfulness and Acceptance Workbook for Anxiety*, New Harbinger Publications Inc., Oakland CA, 2007.

Foster, R. *Celebration of Discipline: The Path to Spiritual Growth*, Harper Collins, San Francisco, 2008.

Gu, J., Strauss, C., Bond, R. and Cavanagh, K. 'How do mindfulness-based cognitive therapy and mindfulness-based stress reduction improve mental health and wellbeing? A systematic review and meta-analysis of meditation studies', *Clinical Psychology Review*, vol. 37, 2015, pp.1–12.

Guy, L. *Introducing Early Christianity: A Topical Survey of its Life, Beliefs and Practices*, IVP, Downers Grove IL, 2004.

Hagner, D.A. *Word Biblical Commentary Matthew 1–13* (vol. 33a), Word Books, Dallas TX, 1993.

Hagner, D.A. *Word Biblical Commentary Matthew 14–28* (vol. 33b), Word Books, Dallas TX, 1995.

Harris, R. *The Happiness Trap*, Exisle Publishing, Wollombi NSW, 2008.

Harris, R. *The Reality Slap*, Exisle Publishing, Wollombi NSW, 2011.

Harris, R. and Aisbett, B. *The Happiness Trap Pocketbook*, Exisle Publishing, Wollombi NSW, 2013.

Hayes, S.C., Luoma, J.B., Bond, F.W., Masuda, A. and Lillis, J. 'Acceptance and commitment therapy: model, processes and outcomes',

Behavior Research and Therapy, vol. 44, no. 1, 2006, pp. 1–25.

Hiebert, P.G. *Anthropological Insights for Missionaries*, Baker Books, Grand Rapids MI, 2004.

Hiebert, P.G., Shaw, R.D. and Tienou, T. *Understanding Folk Religion*, Baker Books, Grand Rapids MI, 2003.

Hoffman, S.G. and Asmundson, G.J.G. 'Acceptance and mindfulness-based therapy: new wave or old hat?', *Clinical Psychology Review*, vol. 28, 2008, pp. 1–16.

Kabat-Zinn, J. 'Mindfulness-based interventions in context: past, present and future', *Clinical Psychology: Science and Practice*, vol. 10, 2003, pp. 144–56.

Kabat-Zinn, J. *Wherever You Go, There You Are: Mindfulness Meditation in Everyday Life*, Hearst Publications, US, 1994.

Kloury, B., Sharma, M., Rush, S.E. and Fournier, C. 'Mindfulness-based stress reduction for healthy individuals: a meta-analysis', *Journal of Psychosomatic Research*, vol. 78, 2015, pp. 519–28.

Kysar, R. *Augsburg Commentary on the New Testament John*, Augsburg Publishing House, Minneapolis MN, 1986.

Lewis, D.C. *After Atheism: Religion and Ethnicity in Russia and Central Asia*, Curzon Press, Richmond UK, 2000.

Linehan, M.M. *Skills Training Manual for Treating Borderline Personality Disorder*, The Guilford Press, New York, 1993.

Mallouhi, C.A. *Miniskirts, Mothers and Muslims: A Christian Woman in a Muslim Land*, Lion Hudson Plc, Oxford UK, 2004.

Merkes, M. 'Mindfulness-based stress reduction for people with chronic diseases', *Australian Journal of Primary Health*, vol. 16, 2010, pp. 200–210.

Merton, T. *New Seeds of Contemplation*, New Directions Books, New York, 2007.

Merton, T. *Thomas Merton – Spiritual Direction and Meditation*, Amazon Digital Services, London, 2013, Kindle edition.

Moltmann, J. *The Source of Life*, SCM Press Ltd, London, 1997.

Moore, A. and Malinowski, P. 'Meditation, mindfulness and cognitive flexibility', *Consciousness and Cognition*, vol. 18, 2009, pp. 176–86.

Morton, J. and Shaw, L. *Wise Choices: Acceptance and Commitment Therapy Groups for People with Borderline Personality Disorder*, Spectrum, Melbourne, 2012.

Nolland, J. *Word Biblical Commentary Luke 1–9:20* (vol. 35a), Word Books, Dallas TX, 1989.

Nolland, J. *Word Biblical Commentary Luke 9:21–18:34* (vol. 35b), Word Books, Dallas TX, 1993.

Ortberg, J. *The Life You've Always Wanted: Spiritual Disciplines for Ordinary People*, Zondervan Publishing House, Grand Rapids MI, 1997.

Ost, L-G. 'Efficacy of the third wave of behavioural therapies: a systematic review and meta-analysis', *Behaviour Research and Therapy*, vol. 46, 2008, pp. 296–321.

Rohr, R. *The Naked Now*, The Crossroad Publishing Company, New York, 2015.

Rubia, K. 'The neurobiology of meditation and its clinical effectiveness in psychiatric disorders', *Biological Psychiatry*, vol. 82, 2009, pp. 1–11.

Sharma, M. and Rush, S.E. 'Mindfulness-based stress reduction as a stress management intervention for healthy individuals: a systematic review', *Journal of Evidence-Based Complementary and Alternative Medicine*, vol. 19, 2014, pp. 271–86.

Smiling Mind. 'Who We Are,' retrieved 25 Nov 2017, https://www.smilingmind.com.au/about/.

Smith, J.B. *The Good and Beautiful God*, IVP, Downers Grove IL, 2009.

St Ignatius of Loyola. *The Spiritual Exercises*, CreateSpace, Charleston, 2012, Kindle edition.

St Patrick. *St Patrick's Breastplate*, Our Catholic Prayers, 2016. Retrieved 25 Nov 2017, http://www.ourcatholicprayers.com/st-patricks-breastplate.html.

Stead, T. *Mindfulness and Christian Spirituality: Making Space for God*, SPCK Publishing, London, 2016.

Strosahl, K.D. and Robinson, P.J. *The Mindfulness and Acceptance Workbook for Depression*, New Harbinger Publications Inc., Oakland CA, 2008.

Sun, J. 'Mindfulness in context: a historical discourse analysis', *Contemporary Buddhism*, vol. 15, no. 2, 2014, pp. 394–415.

Taylor, J.V. *The Go Between God*, SCM Press Ltd, London, 1972.

Teresa of Avila. *Interior Castle*, Image, New York, 2013.

Traub, G. and Mooney, D. *A Biography of St Ignatius Loyola (1491–1556): The Founder of the Jesuits*, The Centre for Mission and Identity, Xavier University, 2016. Retrieved 25 Nov 2017, http://www.xavier.edu/mission-identity/heritage-tradition/who-was-St-Ignatius-Loyola.cfm.

Twenge, J.M. and Campbell, W.K. *The Narcissism Epidemic*, Free Press, New York, 2009.

Unknown. *The Cloud of Unknowing*, in T*op 7 Catholic Classics: On Loving God, The Cloud of Unknowing, Dialogue of Saint Catherine of Siena, The Imitation of Christ, Interior Castle, Dark Night of the Soul, The Practice of the Presence of God* (Top Christian Classics Book 3), Amazon Digital Services, London, 2012, Kindle edition.

van der Velden, A.M., Kuyken, W., Wattar, U., Crane, C., Pallesen, K.J., Dahlgaard, J., Fjorback, L.O. and Piet, J. 'A systematic review of mechanisms of change in mindfulness-based cognitive therapy in the treatment of recurrent major depressive disorder', *Clinical Psychology Review*, vol. 37, 2015, pp. 26–39.

Welch, S. *How to Be a Mindful Christian: 40 Spiritual Practices*, Canterbury Press Norwich, London, 2016.

Willard, D. *Hearing God: Developing a Conversational Relationship with God*, IVP, Downers Grove IL, 2012.